C000142101

DANCE LIKE EVERYBODY'S WATCHING!

DANCE LIKE EVERYBODY'S WATCHING!

THE WEIRD AND WONDERFUL WORLD OF SPORTING MASCOTS

Nick Miller

HarperCollins*Publishers*

This book is not endorsed or sponsored in any way

HarperCollins*Publishers*
1 London Bridge Street
London SE1 9GF
www.harpercollins.co.uk

First published by HarperCollins*Publishers* 2019

10 9 8 7 6 5 4 3 2 1

© Nick Miller 2019

Nick Miller asserts the moral right to be identified
as the author of this work

A catalogue record of this book is available from the
British Library

ISBN 978-0-00-835682-8

Design by Bobby Birchall, Bobby&Co, London
Printed and bound in Latvia

All rights reserved. No part of this publication may be
reproduced, stored in a retrieval system, or transmitted,
in any form or by any means, electronic, mechanical,
photocopying, recording or otherwise, without the prior
written permission of the publishers.

MIX
Paper from
responsible sources
FSC™ C007454

This book is produced from independently certified FSC™ paper
to ensure responsible forest management.

For more information visit: www.harpercollins.co.uk/green

TO THE MEN AND WOMEN
WHO PUT ON GIANT MUPPET SUITS,
WHO SWEAT UNDER SIX INCHES OF
FELT WHEN IT'S 35 DEGREES, WHO ARE
MAULED BY KIDS HOPPED UP ON SUGAR,
WHO POSE FOR ENDLESS PHOTOS TAKEN
BY FRAZZLED PARENTS, WHO GET STUFF
THROWN AT THEIR HEADS AND HAVE
TO BE CHEERFUL THE
WHOLE TIME.

TO THE MASCOTS.

INTRODUCTION

A little while ago I was at an Arsenal game. After the final whistle, as 60,000 people trudged away into the London night, I noticed a gaggle of kids and their parents gathering roughly around where the players would eventually emerge. I assumed they were waiting for pictures and autographs from their footballing heroes, but then, instead of a highly skilled and dedicated athlete, a large, green, furry dinosaur made its way out – and was mobbed.

It turns out the kids were waiting for Gunnersaurus, the friendly anthropomorphised dinosaur that, for reasons that aren't entirely clear, had been adopted as the club's mascot some time earlier.

All of which reminded me that people think watching sport is about, well, watching sport – sitting down and paying attention only to the period of time during which these men or women run around and perform, their otherworldly talents displayed for us to enjoy, gawp and shout at, and, for a special select few, think we could do better.

But it's not really. Well, not entirely. If that were true, nobody would talk, read, write or think about sport except for when the game was actually taking place. We wouldn't wear implausibly expensive merchandise, we wouldn't follow the players on social media, we would probably pay less attention to interviews with the sportsmen and women, and we would most definitely pay more attention to those better voices of our conscience who make the sadly convincing case that it is, in fact, only a game.

It is, however, the ephemera that keep us going. The things that surround sport that don't have much to do with it. The bits that might seem superfluous but give the whole thing a little colour. The sauce on the steak; the steak is the most important bit, naturally, but you wouldn't want it without the sauce.

Things like mascots. Those mostly furry, usually oversized, gaudy characters that prance around the field before, during and after the game, theoretically for the kids to enjoy, but more often than not for the adults to laugh at.

Because, for the most part, these mascots are absurd, surreal concoctions of a dangerous mind, bedraggled rejects from *Sesame Street*, characters they decided were too weird to be a sidekick to Big Bird.

We've had birds, dinosaurs, sheep, cows, fish, worms, tigers, lions, dogs, donkeys, ants, slugs, bats. There have been vegetables, plants, trees, chips, oranges and chillies. Some have tried fur-covered versions of people, aliens and otherworldly made-up creatures that seem to serve no purpose other than to fuel the psychotherapy industry for a generation of scarred youngsters. We've seen hammers, household boilers and planes. And then, the last refuge of the lazy mascot-maker, simply the relevant item of sporting equipment, with added limbs.

Essentially, if someone can figure out how to put legs and arms on something, then it can and probably has been tried as a mascot. In many cases they're strange pieces of performance art, the sort of thing where you daren't even think about the mental process that brought them into being.

Mascots are inherently absurd, but then again you, dear reader, almost certainly dedicate significant portions of your life to teams of men and women that have very little idea that you exist. If you support a team, given how transient the players, coaches, owners and even stadia are, you're essentially cheering laundry, as Seinfeld once put it. And if that's not absurd, then what is?

Which shouldn't be a surprise. After all, fandom is just as illogical as mascots. The whole idea of mascots is based on the hope that something or someone accompanying the team might have some sort of mystical impact on how that team performs. Clearly ludicrous, but for anyone who's had a lucky hat, shirt, jacket, socks or underwear, you know why a mascot is there.

Mascots exist as a reminder that we all take this too seriously. Sport isn't a matter of life and death, and no, it's not more important than that. It is, as the old saying goes, the most important of the unimportant things, but we still need a nudge every now and then to make sure we know it. What better than the sight of a deranged muppet firing T-shirts into a crowd to do that?

And in the end, whether a mascot is ill-conceived or brilliantly designed, they're just supposed to be fun. Which is what watching sport is supposed to be.

This is a celebration of mascots. The worst, the best, the silliest, the most absurd, and everything in between. All of the examples in this book could most charitably be described as ridiculous, but the concept itself is fairly ridiculous, so why not go all-out?

Enjoy.

A BRIEF HISTORY OF MASCOTS

As ever with these things, nobody is sure who or what the first mascot was, the facts lost in the mists of time.

The word 'mascot' itself can be traced back to medieval Latin, in which *masca* meant 'mask' or 'nightmare'. From there it made its way into 18th-century France, where *mascoto* loosely translated to 'witch' or 'sorcerer'. This became a slang word, *mascotte*, essentially referring to a lucky charm or talisman, usually associated with gambling, but the first time it was really applied to sports teams was in the 1880s in the United States.

At that stage these 'mascots' were usually small boys adopted by clubs, which isn't quite as sinister as it sounds. There was a kid named Chic who is mentioned in some books; he was not connected to a specific team, but was regarded as a good-luck charm by some baseball players; the Chicago White Stockings were led in parades by a boy named Willie Hahn, who would hold their flag high; and the St. Louis Brown Stockings were associated with 'Little Nick', whom the *Sporting Life* magazine described as 'the luckiest man in the country', and who supposedly passed on this luck to the team. Sportspeople being inherently superstitious, the idea of anything that could bring a little extra fortune was heartily embraced.

As sports became more organised around the turn of the 20th century, mascots generally became live animals. The oldest mascot is probably Handsome Dan, a bulldog that belonged to a student at Yale in the 1890s, and stuck around: there have been 17 subsequent Dans, the name passed on down the generations of Yale bulldogs, and No. 18 is going strong at the time of writing.

Inevitably, being connected to a university, Handsome Dan has been the subject of various kidnap-related japes, the first coming in 1934 when the editors of *The Harvard Lampoon* abducted him ahead of a big game between the rival institutions. You had to make your own fun back then.

Over the years countless real animals have been used as mascots – horses, pigs, goats, birds, huskies, rams, bears, lions, tigers – some connected to team nicknames, some seemingly entirely random. Plenty have been paraded at games, but some – most notably the tiger and the lion – would probably be regarded as something of a health and safety concern, and are kept to the realms of the conceptual.

All of these examples are from American sports, and it would be easy to assume that the mascot was a concept born and developed in that country, something rather too gaudy for the much more prim and proper English. But it's simply not true. Zampa the Lion, for example, Millwall's mascot named after the road that their stadium is on, has been around for nearly a century, and not just on the club's badge. Zampa has existed in corporeal, furry form for most of that time, at various points looking like a slightly deformed cousin of the lion from *The Wizard of Oz*.

England is also where we find the first mascot for a World Cup. World Cup Willie – a lion dressed in a Union Flag shirt and shorts – was designed in five minutes by an illustrator called Reg Hoye, and also came with a song by skiffle singer Lonnie Donegan. He inspired other tournaments to try their own mascots, but perhaps unsurprisingly 'League Cup Les', attempted a year later, didn't quite capture the country's imagination.

By the 1950s 'character' mascots started to emerge, the first probably being Mr. Oriole, mascot of the Baltimore Orioles, who emerged in around 1954 but soon faded. Not long after came one of the most famous and best loved: Mr. Met, initially just a cartoon character on scorecards for New York Mets games, was fully realised in 1964 when a full-sized, costumed version began making appearances at Shea Stadium. When you explain Mr. Met in mere words – he's a man with a giant baseball for a head – he sounds deeply weird, to say the least, but somehow still works. Although 'retired' for the better part of two decades, he was eventually revived after a campaign by fans in the early 1990s.

A big reason why he was quietly ushered away from the spotlight was the emergence in the 1970s of what we know today as

DANCE LIKE EVERYBODY'S WATCHING!

mascots, the larger-than-life, Muppet-like creatures that you'll see throughout this book.

The San Diego Chicken was the first, initially a promotional character for a radio station called KGB-FM (meaning he was somewhat menacingly known as the 'KGB Chicken' for a spell), but who became adopted by the San Diego Padres when the man who played him decided he wanted to get into games for free. The Chicken, zany antics and all, proved wildly popular, and copycats followed, the most notable being the Phillie Phanatic, broadly regarded as the model for the modern-day mascot.

These days you'll struggle to find a major sports team, tournament or organisation that doesn't have – or hasn't had – a mascot, for better or worse. It's almost a separate industry in itself; with every mascot comes merchandise, personal appearances, commercial endorsements and myriad other money-making schemes. They've come a long way from a dog that some students stole in the name of banter.

NAME **GRITTY**

TEAM **PHILADELPHIA FLYERS**

SPORT **ICE HOCKEY**

YEARS ACTIVE **2018–PRESENT**

STYLE FROM **THE WRONG SIDE OF THE TRACKS TO SESAME STREET**

FAMOUS FOR **THREATENING TO MURDER ANOTHER MASCOT IN ITS SLEEP**

The Philadelphia Flyers had gone 42 years without a mascot, until they decided in 2018 that they could no longer be left out of the game and thus introduced a waking nightmare into the consciousness of America.

If *The Muppets* ever changed direction and told the story of a quiet loner who lived in a remote cabin and ate wolves while they were still alive, they would cast Gritty in the lead role. A bug-eyed orange monster with a beard, Gritty would look very at home with a rifle over his shoulder and the entrails of a rival flecked around his fur.

The thing is, though, it seems to be working. A Flyers suit once noted that Gritty would match the 'blue-collar nature of the Philadelphia fanbase', and after the whole of America recoiled in horror at whatever this thing was, the good people of Philly closed ranks behind their boy. He was one of theirs now. And when the Pittsburgh Penguins mascot (a penguin, as it happens) tweeted a gentle jibe in his direction, Gritty replied, 'Sleep with one eye open, bird.' If nothing else, the good people of Philadelphia appreciate a mascot who will murder another to defend their honour.

NAME GUNNERSAURUS REX

TEAM **ARSENAL**

SPORT **FOOTBALL**

YEARS ACTIVE **1994–PRESENT**

STYLE **BIG, GREEN, GOOFY, AND A DINOSAUR THAT INEXPLICABLY LIVES IN NORTH LONDON**

FAMOUS FOR **IMPECCABLY OBSERVING MINUTE'S SILENCES**

It's easy to make fun of Gunnersaurus. Broadly because, well, it's easy to make fun of him. He's a giant green dinosaur that's the mascot for a team in a very urban area of north London, with wide, vacant eyes and a big stupid grin. He has a long neck on which he seems to wear a choker with an Arsenal badge, which makes him seem a bit like a 14-year-old girl in around 1999. He looks like Barney's long-lost cousin who was exiled from the family after clumsily knocking over a vase one too many times. Very little about him makes sense.

But there's a very sweet story behind Gunnersaurus. The club ran a competition to design their mascot back in 1994 and it was won by 11-year-old Peter Lovell, who at the time thought up the dinosaur idea because he a) was obsessed with *Jurassic Park* and b) thought it represented 'the ferocity and power of Arsenal Football Club'. Stop laughing at the back there. Anyway, 20 years later Peter got married, and who should make an appearance at his wedding but Gunnersaurus himself, bringing gifts from the club including a letter from then manager Arsène Wenger.

Gunnersaurus is undoubtedly the most well-known mascot in football, so by that measure he's obviously been a huge success. And he really is the best representative of mascots in the game, in that he's inherently absolutely ridiculous, something most clearly displayed when he solemnly observes minute's silences along with the Arsenal players.

DANCE LIKE EVERYBODY'S WATCHING!

NAME **POE**

TEAM **BALTIMORE RAVENS**

SPORT **AMERICAN FOOTBALL**

YEARS ACTIVE **1998–PRESENT**

STYLE **A WINNING COMBINATION OF CUDDLY, CHILD-FRIENDLY AND MURDEROUS**

FAMOUS FOR **BEING NAMED AFTER A DARK 19TH-CENTURY WRITER**

The Baltimore Ravens must have been in a bit of a bind when coming up with their mascot. It could hardly be anything other than a raven: the whole endeavour would have been a laughing stock if they'd gone off-piste and picked a lion or an otter or something. The problem being that ravens are inherently sinister creatures, associated more with lurking in the roofs of abandoned houses than being cuddly and loveable, which isn't exactly the vibe you want from a character designed to entertain children.

The team is named after Baltimore resident Edgar Allan Poe's poem 'The Raven', and in turn a couple of years after the team was established they unveiled not one but three mascots, all ravens, named Edgar, Allan and Poe. This merely added to Poe's sinisterness, however, as in 2008 the other two were 'retired', which makes it sound very much like they were 'retired' by a ruthless sibling. But not to worry: they were replaced by two actual, live ravens, named 'Rise' and 'Conquer', which naturally made the trio much less terrifying.

Let's not dance around this one. At some point – it may not be today, it may not be tomorrow or the day after – the chances are that Poe will kill us all in our sleep, while his sidekicks Rise and Conquer keep watch. We all must make our peace with this.

NAME **SAMMY THE SHRIMP**

TEAM **SOUTHEND UNITED**

SPORT **FOOTBALL**

YEARS ACTIVE **c.1980–PRESENT**

STYLE **BLISSED-OUT SEAFOOD ON THE ENGLISH COAST**

FAMOUS FOR **GETTING INVOLVED IN A TEAM INJURY CRISIS**

They had a bit of a rethink about the Sammy the Shrimp costume recently. Just as well, really. Whichever way you sliced it, however generously you thought of it, no matter how pure you thought their intentions, it was difficult to look at the old Sammy with his tall, pointy head and see anything but a pink Ku Klux Klan hood. It was not, to say the least, the best look.

Now Sammy's bonce has been rounded a little more, and he looks normal. Well, not normal: he's a giant shrimp who dances around the football pitch in a town near the seaside in the south of England. There's not much normal about that. It's also pretty funny that they replaced Sammy's previously quite human-looking hands with some more shrimpy pincers. You know, for realism's sake.

Sammy has been an integral part of the Southend family for some time, but he took things to another level in 2018 when he – or at least the man inside the shrimp costume – became involved in an injury crisis, joining ten players in the treatment room after damaging a disc in his back. Don't worry, though. He got treatment from the club physiotherapist and was back in action shortly afterwards.

DANCE LIKE EVERYBODY'S WATCHING!

NAME **WALLY**

TEAM **BOSTON RED SOX**

SPORT **BASEBALL**

YEARS ACTIVE **1997—PRESENT**

STYLE **FRIEND TO THE CHILDREN, ENEMY TO THE GRUMPY NATIVES**

FAMOUS FOR **SUPPOSEDLY LIVING INSIDE THE LEFT-FIELD WALL AT FENWAY PARK**

Boston sports fans have a reputation for being . . . how to put this . . . salty. No nonsense. Bad tempered, even. So you can imagine the reception when, on opening day of the 1997 season, a 6ft-tall green cuddly toy emerged onto the field at Fenway Park to throw the ceremonial first pitch.

Fenway is famous for the giant wall in left field, latterly known as the 'Green Monster'. So you can imagine the brainstorming meeting the Red Sox bods had when trying to come up with a concept for their new family-friendly, cuddly mascot. 'So you're saying we have a WALL, called the GREEN MONSTER in our park . . . I have no idea what we should call our mascot, nor what colour he should be or the type of creature.'

Actually, what they lacked in originality for the name, they made up for in back story. Wally had supposedly lived in the Green Monster since 1947, which, given he was introduced to a semi-enthusiastic public in 1997, meant he had just been sitting there doing nothing for 50 years. Pretty creepy. Still, Red Sox stalwart and broadcaster Jerry Remy has written five whole books about the adventures of Wally, plus he has a drink at Dunkin' Donuts named after him and once featured in a specifically commissioned cartoon. None of which has stopped the locals using language that would make a docker blush about him, though.

NAME **H'ANGUS THE MONKEY**

TEAM **HARTLEPOOL UNITED**

SPORT **FOOTBALL**

YEARS ACTIVE **1999–PRESENT**

STYLE **CROSS-EYED REJECT FROM *PLANET OF THE APES***

FAMOUS FOR **BEING ELECTED AS MAYOR OF HARTLEPOOL**

Most mascots have a concocted back story, but the origin tale of H'Angus the Monkey is darker than most. The residents of Hartlepool are breezily known in some quarters as 'monkey hangers', something based on an old myth that, when a French ship ran aground near the town during the Napoleonic Wars, the only survivor was a monkey that the crew had dressed in a sailor's uniform. Having seen neither a Frenchman nor a monkey before, the people of the town supposedly assumed the creature was a French spy, and it was duly hanged.

Thus, H'Angus the Monkey. Cheery stuff. Perhaps with this grim tale in mind, H'Angus developed a reputation for 'anarchic' behaviour, which included but was not limited to simulating copulation with a female steward, and being kicked out of Blackpool's ground amid suspicion he had taken drink.

Sounds like a perfect elected official, right? Well, yes, as it turned out. In 2002 all the established political parties were jostling to become the first directly elected mayor of Hartlepool, so Stewart Drummond, the man playing H'Angus at the time, decided to run as 'a laugh' and to drum up a little publicity for the club. But, in an early sign that mainstream politics was about to get very silly indeed, he won. And not only did he win, but he was elected twice more before the post was abolished in 2013. Sadly, he did not govern as the monkey.

NAME **DINGER**

TEAM **COLORADO ROCKIES**

SPORT **BASEBALL**

YEARS ACTIVE **1994–PRESENT**

STYLE **A CROSS BETWEEN A TRICERATOPS AND A TELETUBBY**

FAMOUS FOR **BEING 'BORN' OUT OF A DINOSAUR EGG ON THE FIELD**

Sometimes you just have to take your hat off. The Colorado Rockies are a relatively new organisation, playing their first Major League Baseball game in 1993, and had to rent a stadium while their own was being built. During construction, workers found a number of dinosaur fossils on the site, most notably a large triceratops skull. This also happened to be around the time the Rockies were deciding on their new mascot, so in some ways they were offered no choice.

And thus, Dinger was born. For those of you not familiar with baseball slang, 'Dinger' might sound like a slightly risqué name for a gentleman's personal area, but it is in fact slang for 'home run', and since Coors Field, the aforementioned fossil-hosting home of the Rockies, is about 5,200 feet above sea level and the thin air makes it easier to hit the ball very, very far, the name of their mascot becomes obvious too.

What isn't quite so obvious is the way Dinger – a version of Barney the Dinosaur, but with the wide, vacant eyes of someone who has just been smacked in the head with a plank of wood – was introduced to the world. On the field before a game, Dinger emerged from a giant egg, helped by two 'doctors', who, and call us cynical here, we suspect did not have the relevant medical qualifications, then proceeded to stumble around the place like, well, someone who's just been smacked in the head with a plank of wood. The thing is Barn . . . sorry, Dinger, just doesn't really do anything. He's not fun. He's not intimidating. He's not even that cuddly. He is, in the words of one fan, 'a bit of a dweeb'.

NAME **GILBERT THE GULL**

TEAM **TORQUAY UNITED**

SPORT **FOOTBALL**

YEARS ACTIVE **1977–PRESENT**

STYLE **HAPPY-GO-LUCKY GULL, BUT WITH A BIT OF A TEMPER**

FAMOUS FOR **ALLEGEDLY CALLING HIS OWN FANS A VERY BAD WORD INDEED**

On the face of things, there's nothing that unusual about Gilbert the Gull, mascot of Torquay United, perennial strugglers in the lowest tiers of the English football pyramid. He's a large, colourful, furry representation of the club's nickname who goofs around on the touchline before games. So far, so standard.

However, this Gull apparently has a bit of . . . edge to him. In 2014 Torquay were playing Grimsby Town and the atmosphere among their fans wasn't exactly convivial, given they were being handed a sound thrashing. Gilbert went over to ask where the noise had gone, one thing led to another and he – allegedly – ended up calling his own fans a bad word. The big, bad word. Yes, *that* big, bad word.

'He called us a "bunch of c***s",' complained one fan, 'and after a few words were exchanged he waddled off back to the Family Stand.' Another fan added: 'The mascot was – and no doubt about it – telling fans to come onto the pitch for a fight.' Steve Jegat, the man who played Gilbert at the time, denied dropping the C-bomb, but he was temporarily suspended from duties by the club. 'Gilbert has been spoken to,' solemnly intoned the club's chief executive, and the fact he said 'Gilbert' rather than 'Steve' conjures up the delicious image of the Gull, in full costume, sitting forlornly in an office somewhere as he's being given a stern talking-to.

NAME **KING CAKE BABY**

TEAM **NEW ORLEANS PELICANS**

SPORT **BASKETBALL**

YEARS ACTIVE **2009–PRESENT**

STYLE **GIGANTIC, LAMINATED CHILD'S DOLL BROUGHT TO HORRIFYING LIFE**

FAMOUS FOR **POSSIBLY BEING THE INSPIRATION FOR A CHARACTER IN THE FILM *HAPPY DEATH DAY***

If you've ever seen *Toy Story 3*, it's OK to admit that Big Baby, one of the film's primary villains, along with the bitter and twisted Lotso, is pretty scary. Why wouldn't you find a doll with a lazy eye brought to life who threatens Andy, Buzz and chums just a little bit intimidating? Well, if you were a little alarmed by one of Pixar's more unsettling creations, visiting the New Orleans Pelicans NBA team is probably not recommended.

This particular inspiration for nightmares is born from a local tradition in which a small doll is hidden inside a limited number of king cakes – doughy, ring-shaped items of confectionery – around Mardi Gras time, with whoever finds the doll being granted good luck. While that raises a number of health and safety/choking-related issues, more terrifying than the prospect of getting some plastic caught in your gullet is this thing, who looks like it sustains itself on the pulsating fear from anyone it looks at with its bug eyes, growing stronger and stronger as you become more and more terrified.

A couple of years ago the creator of King Cake Baby sued the producers of the film *Happy Death Day* on the grounds that he believed the mask worn by the killer in that film was inspired by the mascot. Which does rather lead to the question: if your creation designed to entertain the youngsters of New Orleans could plausibly be a movie mass-murderer, is it worth a rethink?

NAME **ALFRED G.RILLA**

TEAM **GLOUCESTERSHIRE**

SPORT **CRICKET**

YEARS ACTIVE **2015–PRESENT**

STYLE **THE SOFT, FLUFFY VERSION OF A REAL, STUFFED GORILLA**

FAMOUS FOR **WINNING THE MASCOT DERBY TWO YEARS IN A ROW**

Alfred the Gorilla is a Bristol institution. Now, before we go any further we should establish that there are two Alfred the Gorillas. There's the real Alfred, an actual gorilla that lived/was held captive (depending on your point of view) at Bristol Zoo from 1930 to 1948, was stuffed after his death and remains on display to this very day. And then there's the mascot Alfred, the ape who represents Gloucestershire County Cricket Club, and constantly looks as if he's just asked to borrow a fiver and is trying to persuade you to hand it over.

Now, a friendly looking gorilla does seem like a pretty good idea for a mascot. Who doesn't like a gorilla? Except those biplane pilots that King Kong swatted out of the air, obviously, but let's not get bogged down in that. But we can't help thinking that the other version of Alfred would make for a decent mascot too. Nobody has thought of that. Just get the stuffed, real Alfred in and sit him by the side of the field. Imagine how intimidating that would be. 'Don't mess with these guys – they've brought a stuffed gorilla, they must be absolutely insane.'

As it is, the animated version of Alfred is doing OK, particularly in the field of athletic achievement. Every year on cricket's Twenty20 finals day there's a mascot race, where representatives of all the clubs chase around the outfield and more often than not trip over in various entertaining ways. And Alfred won that race two years in a row, in 2016 and 2017. Sure, the stuffed Alfred possibly wouldn't be able to do that . . . but you never know.

NAMES GLIZ AND NEVE

EVENT **WINTER OLYMPICS**

YEAR ACTIVE **2006**

STYLE **A REPRESENTATION OF COLD THINGS . . . BECAUSE THE WINTER OLYMPICS ARE COLD**

FAMOUS **FOR BEING PROBABLY THE LEAST IMAGINATIVE MASCOTS IN SPORTS HISTORY**

If you're familiar with Alan Partridge, you'll know the scene in which he's pitching TV-show ideas to the controller of BBC Light Entertainment. After scrolling through a number of unsuitable premises, Partridge, bereft of inspiration, shrugs and says, '. . . monkey tennis?' We can only imagine that's how Gliz and Neve came to be mascots for the 2006 Winter Olympics in Turin, the only difference being that in Partridge, his barrel-scraping idea was turned down.

Gliz and Neve were – and we promise we're not making this up – an ice cube and a snowball. Because it's cold in winter, right? And what could be colder than an ice cube and a snowball! Nothing! Go cold things!

Naturally, their existence was explained by some honking marketing nonsense, the organisers explaining that they represented 'the spirit of the Italian Olympic event: passion, enthusiasm, culture, elegance, and love of the environment and of sport'. Look, just admit you realised two weeks before the Games started that you'd forgotten to sort a mascot, so just panicked and put in an order for the first two cold things you could think of.

NAME **HUGO THE HORNET**

TEAM **CHARLOTTE HORNETS**

SPORT **BASKETBALL**

YEARS ACTIVE **1988—PRESENT**

STYLE **AN INSECT THAT LOOKS LIKE IT BUYS ITS CLOTHES AT GAP**

FAMOUS FOR **BEING ACCIDENTALLY NAMED AFTER A HURRICANE THAT KILLED 34 PEOPLE**

The Charlotte Hornets did the democratic thing when it came to naming their mascot, back in 1988. Around 6,000 people responded to their invitation to suggest a moniker for this fuzzy, buzzy ball of insecty fun, and in the end alliteration won the day. Hugo it was. Unfortunately, a few months later, and while their new mascot was still to gain a foothold in the national consciousness, Hurricane Hugo hit Puerto Rico and the south-eastern coast of America, wreaking havoc and causing 34 fatalities. Unfortunate timing, to say the least.

Ultimately the team did the sensible thing and reasoned that nobody could credibly make a connection between the two, and thus stuck with the name the people had settled on. Hugo stayed with the team when they moved to New Orleans in 2004, but returned to Charlotte when the New Orleans team renamed themselves the Pelicans, and the Charlotte Bobcats changed to the Charlotte Hornets. Confusing.

Still, Hugo – designed by Cheryl Henson, daughter of mascot patron saint Jim – remains a constant, buzzing away in colours that are probably supposed to be bright and psychedelic, but actually just look like he shops in the summer T-shirts section of Gap. Maybe in an attempt to spice up his image, Hugo once jumped through a ring of fire to dunk a basketball, but unfortunately nobody could work out how to extinguish the fire, then when they eventually did they managed to spread chemicals all over the court, leading to a long delay in the game. Hugo stood by, looking embarrassed.

DANCE LIKE EVERYBODY'S WATCHING!

NAME **ROBBIE THE BOBBY**

TEAM **BURY**

SPORT **FOOTBALL**

YEARS ACTIVE **1997–2018**

STYLE **AN OVERLY AGGRESSIVE POLICEMAN, IF YOU CAN BELIEVE THAT**

FAMOUS FOR **BEING SENT OFF THREE TIMES IN ONE SEASON**

There isn't a lot in Bury. There hasn't ever really been a lot in Bury, a fairly grim satellite town of Manchester, and there's never been a lot from Bury. What they do have is Robert Peel, the man who created the Metropolitan Police in 1829, who was born there back in 1788. So when it came to deciding on a mascot, he seemed the obvious inspiration, and thus Robbie the Bobby was born.

It's somewhat ironic, therefore, that Robbie found himself on the wrong side of the law so frequently. In his heyday, Robbie was quite the hellraiser, sent off three times in one season once for assorted misdemeanours, including but not limited to tearing the ears off Peterborough's rabbit mascot and rather forcibly removing the head of Bartley the Bluebird from Cardiff. Jonathan Pollard, the man who 'played' Robbie for a spell, was eventually sacked after making obscene gestures towards referee Howard Webb during a game, and responded to the repeated scrapes he got involved in by saying, 'They start it and I finish it.'

Robbie eventually calmed down a bit, but sadly was replaced in 2018 when the club realised that something a little cuter might be in order. Sticking with the legal theme, the new mascot was called Peeler, the police dog. Because there have never been any problems with those in the past . . .

DANCE LIKE EVERYBODY'S WATCHING!

DAVE RAYMOND – THE ORIGINAL

If there is a single most important person in the mascot business, it's Dave Raymond. In the late 1970s he became the Phillie Phanatic, one of the first mascots to assume the furry-costumed form as we know it today. Dave was the Phanatic until the early 1990s, and since then he has built a hugely successful business as a mascot consultant; if you see a mascot in American sports, the chances are he was involved with it, most successfully the Philadelphia Flyers mascot and media sensation 'Gritty'.

He's also a motivational speaker, with a speech entitled 'The Power of Fun' in which he explains how simply choosing to have fun helped him overcome some of the darkest periods of his life.

How did you come to be the Phillie Phanatic?

At college I just wanted to play football and then be a football coach. I got a summer job with the Phillies working for promotions and marketing, all the silliness that was going on in and around the team. I was having a blast and thought, 'Hey, this might be better than being a football coach.' In 1978 they said, 'You can keep your day job . . . we just want you to also stay for all the games,' but they didn't tell me what they wanted me to do right away. They told me I needed to go to New York to get fitted for 'the costume'. I was kind of confused, like, 'What do you mean?' 'Well, the mascot,' they replied. I thought, 'Well, maybe if I do whatever it is they ask me to do, then I'll show them I'd be a valuable employee.' So, that's how it all got started.

What did mascots look like before the Phanatic?

One of the reasons why they created the Phanatic was that there was a character called 'The Chicken' in San Diego. He was the new age of mascots, meaning that the mascot actually entertained fans. Prior to that they were pretty much lumbering, big-headed, cumbersome mascots that didn't move around a lot: they would wave and take photographs, and then disappear.

The Phillies' mascots at the time were called Phil and Phillis, who were two children's characters from the era of the American Revolution

– they wore your typical breeches with boots or buckled shoes, and then they had a big, almost wooden or plaster of Paris bell-shaped body that their arms went out of. Although they were lumbering, like cumbersome robots, they were cute. But they were just visual, and all they did was walk out for the national anthem, then turn around and come back in.

Was any of what you did out on the field planned?

The Phanatic's personality was really directed in my head as a mash-up of the typical Phillies fan and Three Stooges/Daffy Duck-style slapstick comedy. I wanted it to be frenetic because he looked big and heavy, so if I was impetuous and nimble – which I knew I could be in the costume because it wasn't that cumbersome – that would surprise everyone.

The first night I was told, 'Go out with the ground staff in the fifth inning. I don't care what you do, just look like you're working with them.' And, by accident, I tripped one of them and they fell, which got a big laugh, so that grew into this whole routine in the fifth inning, which remains today.

We started building on those routines and different music: when Devo's 'Whip It' was big we came out wearing chains. There was a phone right behind the dugouts, and Bill Giles [then Phillies owner] called me and just said, 'Don't ever do that again. I don't want to micromanage you, but I want to trust you. You've got to remember, we've got kids here.'

The Phanatic famously got into a long-running feud with Tommy Lasorda, the former manager of the LA Dodgers. Was he playing along with it or was he genuinely annoyed with you?

Tommy was a complicated guy. On one hand he was one of the most respected ambassadors of American baseball. On the other hand he had a big ego, just like anybody in his position. One of his players, Rick Sutcliffe, famously said that 90 per cent of people hate him, the other 10 per cent just don't know him.

I'd always made fun of him because he was a kind of a portly guy, bow-legged and pigeon-toed, which is almost physically impossible. So I'd go behind him and try to walk like him. I'd stick my belly out, and the fans just went crazy. He played up to it, and always looked like he was angry – he would pull the Phanatic's tongue out, hand it to one of the fans and people would cheer. So we played it up.

Whenever the Dodgers came to town, I would just constantly make fun of him. Everything he did, I made fun of. For the most part he'd play along, but then the Dodgers players started getting me his uniform so I could dress up a dummy I had. I found out that he wasn't very happy when I found out he told the clubhouse manager, 'Don't bring extra jerseys of mine on the road, because somebody's getting the jersey to the Phanatic.'

So I made a jersey, one that looked exactly like his jersey. That eventually got him to the point where he was so irritable one night he'd just had enough. He came running out and tried to beat the piss out of me. And he really was beating the piss out of me. Then he said in the newspaper the next day that the Phanatic's violence is not good for kids.

You stopped being the Phanatic in 1993, but you stayed in the mascot game. What do you do now?

I felt I needed to find out something that could pay the bills where I wasn't in costume. So eventually I set up Raymond Entertainment with the thought, 'I'm going to help people do this right. I'm going to teach them what the Phillies taught me.'

I tell them what to do [in order to create a new mascot], how to be prepared, the things that they should spend money on, things that they should spend time and focus on, the things that they should stay away from, and then I basically hold their hand through that process. I'm an expert in character branding.

Then there's the Mascot Hall of Fame, which is mostly legacy for me. I want this place to work because it's a place that honours mascots.

And finally, I do speaking. I have my talk called 'The Power of Fun', which I did as a TED talk, and people tell me how important it has been to them. One person said, 'I was an 9/11 responder – I wish I'd heard this speech the day after 9/11.' A young high-school girl came up to me, like she was telling me something mundane her life, and said, 'You know, I've been thinking about suicide lately, but I don't think I'm going to think about that anymore because I really enjoyed your talk.'

NAME **SIR SAINT**

TEAM **NEW ORLEANS SAINTS**

SPORT **AMERICAN FOOTBALL**

YEARS ACTIVE **1967—PRESENT**

STYLE **IF DICK DASTARDLY SUFFERED AN AWFUL SWELLING ALLERGIC REACTION TO SOMETHING**

FAMOUS FOR **ALMOST TOPPLING OVER DAILY DUE TO WEIGHT OF CHIN**

The New Orleans Saints have two mascots: one is Gumbo, a St Bernard dog, which makes a whole lot of sense – he looks friendly, appealing for the children, and the St Bernard parish is partly in New Orleans. But then they have this other guy, Sir Saint, who looks like a caricature of Jay Leno if you squeezed him into a helmet and uniform.

The original logo of the team, Sir Saint mercifully only existed on paper until 2008, when he was brought to hideous 3D life in the form of this giant-chinned mascot, a veritable Dick Dastardly in the midst of a terrible allergic reaction. The brainchild of former Saints owner John Mecom, Sir Saint lay dormant for a couple of decades after being used in the team's logo from the late 1960s to 1984, before being revived and brought to life, and frankly why wouldn't you bring back a character who really should be in *American Dad*?

The thing is, he doesn't really seem to do a great deal either. At least Gumbo can provide some entertainment – after all, he's a big, cuddly dog, and who doesn't love big, cuddly dogs? But Sir Saint's main task appears to be just maintaining his balance, lest that cumbersome chin send him crashing to the floor.

NAME **POACHER THE IMP**

TEAM **LINCOLN CITY**

SPORT **FOOTBALL**

YEARS ACTIVE **1998–PRESENT**

STYLE **RESEMBLING A VERY BADLY SUNBURNT WOMBLE**

FAMOUS FOR **BEING NAMED AFTER A CHEESE**

Plenty of mascots endure sticky starts to life in the cuddly suit, but Poacher the Imp, mascot of Lincoln City, had the misfortune to be introduced just as the club was going through a significant financial crisis. There followed a backlash from supporters angry that the club might be wasting resources on this curious bright red, bearded fellow, who looks like Great Uncle Bulgaria from *The Wombles* if he fell asleep on the beach. Once it was pointed out that the man who played Poacher was not being paid, everyone calmed down a little.

Lincoln's nickname comes from a centuries-old local legend that stated two imps were sent by Satan to run amok, but one of them was turned to stone during a stop at Lincoln Cathedral (it's a lovely tourist spot) and remains there to this day. So their mascot was always going to be an imp, but although 'poacher' is something that has roots in various aspects of Lincoln history, the most prominent is the local cheese. The combination of dairy produce and a satanic messenger was always going to be a winner.

Poacher has got himself into the usual scrapes over the years, including being warned by the police after making an 'unfriendly' gesture towards some Scunthorpe fans, plus being punched by a giddy Sunderland fan after an FA Cup game years back. It's that fiery personality born from hell's depths that does it. That, or the cheese.

NAME **HIP HOP THE RABBIT**

TEAM **PHILADELPHIA 76ERS**

SPORT **BASKETBALL**

YEARS ACTIVE **1997–2011**

STYLE **COOL, OR AT LEAST WHAT MEN IN SUITS WHO ONCE WATCHED AN LL COOL J VIDEO THINK IS COOL**

FAMOUS FOR **SLAM DUNKS, IN VARIOUS FORMS OF COMPLEXITY**

Those of you familiar with *The Simpsons* will recall the episode where the creators of *Itchy & Scratchy*, the cartoon within the cartoon, decided they needed to freshen up their image and appeal to 'the youth'. They came up with a new character called Poochie, who was a dog in sunglasses and a backwards baseball cap. Poochie rapped. Poochie had a skateboard. Poochie was supposed to be a satire on what happens when old, out-of-touch types try to create something 'cool'.

And so to Hip Hop the Rabbit, who for a few years was the mascot of the Philadelphia 76ers. You can see the similarities. In some ways you have to admire the brazenness of this team ignoring any art or pretence about what they were trying to do and just naming this mascot 'Hip Hop'.

And even if it weren't a clumsy attempt to 'get down with the kids', Hip Hop would be bloody terrifying. Because for some reason this bunny is hench, stacked, jacked and muscular, looking – for reasons that remain unclear – just like the nightmarish imaginary rabbit from *Donnie Darko* if he'd spent a year pumping iron and eating whey protein.

Hip Hop's big claims to fame were his increasingly elaborate slam dunks, performed on the court, as well as a sidekick called Lil Hip Hop and a selection of helpers known as the 'Hare Raisers'. Hip Hop was quietly ushered off to the great warren in the sky, although the 76ers seemingly just hoped nobody would notice, as they didn't actually confirm he was no more for another four years.

NAME IYOKANTA

TEAM **EHIME FC**

SPORT **FOOTBALL**

YEARS ACTIVE **2004–PRESENT**

STYLE **AN ORANGE, BUT ABSOLUTELY FURIOUS FOR SOME REASON**

FAMOUS FOR **BEING AN ABSOLUTELY FURIOUS ORANGE**

It cannot be understated how much Japan loves a mascot. Gloriously, unironically, guiltlessly. There are so many examples that we could fill a whole book exclusively with them, but in the interests of brevity let's stick to a few, and one of the finest belongs to Ehime FC, among the more modest football teams in the land. Perhaps it's that modesty that has made Iyokanta so absolutely furious: the clenched teeth, the angry eyes, the leaf atop his head swept to one side that makes it look like he's fighting against a wind of apoplexy.

Maybe this is a deliberate decision by the club, to have a mascot who will almost certainly hunt both you and your family down if you dare beat them. Picture the scene: after a well-earned victory, you're lying in bed at home, satisfied with the day's work, confident you're progressing. Suddenly there's a knock on the window, you tense up, a terrible realisation chills your soul, you pull back the curtains and . . . that incandescent orange is there, waiting, watching.

Iyokanta's origins are fairly obvious – the club is in a citrus-growing region – but he also has sidekicks: Mikan-chan is a lady companion (no word as to whether they're anything more than just friends) and Iyo Kahn is an elder statesman, a wise old figure named in part, for reasons a little unclear, after former Germany goalkeeper Oliver Kahn.

NAMES **ATO, KAZ AND NIK**

EVENT **WORLD CUP**

SPORT **FOOTBALL**

YEAR ACTIVE **2002**

STYLE **COMPUTER-GENERATED, MULTI-COLOURED SPRITES FROM THE FUTURE**

FAMOUS FOR **BEING THE SECOND-MOST RIDICULOUS THING AT THE 2002 WORLD CUP, AFTER BRAZILIAN RONALDO'S HAIR**

Collectively known as 'The Spheriks' (short for 'Atmospheriks'), Ato, Kaz and Nik were apparently part of a group who 'lived in the sky in a place called Atmozone, where they play their own version of football, Atmoball'. Not only were these three imagined as real-life, tangible mascots, but a total of 26 – *twenty-six!* – episodes of a cartoon about their antics were commissioned, spanning 13 – *thirteen!* – hours! Now, Fifa are an organisation not shy of a vanity project, but 26 – *twenty-six!* – episodes! 13 – *thirteen!* – hours!

As for the little chaps themselves, they sort of look like creatures you'd find skulking in the background of the cantina at the start of *Star Wars*. They wouldn't get involved in any aggravation because they're clearly blissed out on some sort of niche street drug that makes the taker sit on the beanbags in the corner of the room and spend the evening giggling.

This is another example of some marketing wonks trying desperately to appeal to The Youth, and coming up with what they think kids would be interested in. You can imagine the pitch: 'It's like, football, but in space. Cool, right, fellow kids?' Absolutely not.

NAME **TOMMY 'THUNDA' POWER**

TEAM **PORT ADELAIDE POWER**

SPORT **AUSTRALIAN RULES FOOTBALL**

YEARS ACTIVE **2003–PRESENT**

STYLE **SUPPOSEDLY TERRIFYING, ACTUALLY LOOKS TERRIFIED**

FAMOUS FOR **BEING A METAPHOR FOR AUSTRALIAN MASCULINITY. POSSIBLY**

If you call your mascot 'Thunda', then you can't really get away with being anything except scary, intimidating, the sort of character who's going to rain down almighty hellfire onto any opponent that has the cheek to cross your path. We're sure that's what Port Adelaide – nicknamed 'Power', presumably by someone who was trying to compensate for something – were going for, but it is rather compromised by a number of key details.

Those eyebrows, for a start. Upturned in surprise, they transform something that could be quite intimidating and alpha into a slightly surprised, vaguely inquisitive, even quite camp expression. And when you combine them with those tightly gritted teeth, it just looks like Tommy has been kidnapped and is being forced to do this. He might as well be holding a copy of today's newspaper and saying, 'My captors are treating me well, but please, do as they ask.'

Maybe all of this is just a comment on the nature of Australian masculinity, or all masculinity. You have the outward symbol of bravado, the lighting bolt, all power and aggression. But along with that you have the terrified expression of a man who is actually extremely vulnerable and who could reveal all sorts of hidden depths if only he had someone – anyone – to talk to. It's a theory. It's almost certainly nonsense. But it's a theory.

NAME CRAZY CRAB

TEAM SAN FRANCISCO GIANTS

SPORT BASEBALL

YEAR ACTIVE 1984

STYLE AN ATTEMPT AT SATIRISING THE FLUFFY MASCOT CRAZE OF THE EARLY 1980s

FAMOUS FOR BEING PELTED WITH GOLF BALLS AND URINE-FILLED BALLOONS

The San Francisco Giants were bad in 1984. And obviously when a team is bad, people are less inclined to show up and buy tickets. So the marketing department thought up a fine wheeze – in response to the rise of furry, Muppetesque mascots like the Phillie Phanatic and San Diego Chicken, they would film a TV commercial with an intentionally terrible mascot, a large crab with stick-on, googly eyes called the 'Crazy Crab'.

Commercial filmed and aired, they figured that since they had the suit, and someone to wear it – a classically trained actor and mime artist named Wayne Doba – they might as well try him out at the ballpark. The Crazy Crab was supposed to be an anti-mascot, designed for people to hate, part comment on the nature of other mascots, part attempt to drum up any kind of emotion at all in their fanbase.

The trouble was, it worked too well. Fans started pelting the Crab with things, initially hot dogs and popcorn, but soon escalating to golf balls, baseballs, batteries and . . . oh God . . . water balloons filled with urine. It got to the point where Doba's suit had to be reinforced with a steel plate in the back and he wore a crash helmet underneath it.

One day a San Diego Padres player took things a little far and tackled the Crab with such force that he injured Doba's back, at which point the Giants called the whole thing to a close and retired the Crab, although he's occasionally been revived since. Doba successfully sued the Padres, but more importantly he and the Giants learned a valuable lesson: if you tell sports fans to hate something, they'll do so – and how.

NAME JÜNTER

TEAM **BORUSSIA MÖNCHENGLADBACH**

SPORT **FOOTBALL**

YEARS ACTIVE **1965–PRESENT**

STYLE **THEORETICALLY A FOAL, BUT LOOKS LIKE A BUG-EYED COW WITH A MOHICAN**

FAMOUS FOR **BEING MANHANDLED BY FORMER US GOALKEEPER KASEY KELLER**

If you want longevity and loyalty, you've come to the right place here. Jünter, a giant black and white horse with demented eyes and a mohican, who actually looks more like a giant black and white cow with demented eyes and a mohican, has been around in various forms since 1965. Apparently named after Günter Netzer, probably the greatest player in Borussia's history, a horse was chosen because the club had acquired the nickname 'The Foals' as a result of the number of young players in the team.

But, ironically, his current incarnation looks like it would terrify any youngsters that came near him. Maybe that's why former Borussia goalkeeper Kasey Keller had a running war with Jünter, engaging in various forms of – wait for it – horseplay with the equine japester, including lifting him up onto his shoulders and bodyslamming him after a game in 2005. 'I'm picking him up, soft-slamming him and putting him over my knee, elbow smashing him,' chuckled Keller a few years later, 'and then I pin him, it was insane. It went all over Germany.'

Incidentally, if you were so inclined, you can buy a Jünter blanket to keep you warm on cold winter evenings. Well, we say 'blanket'; it's actually a piece of synthetic-looking material with the head and feet of Jünter, making it look more like a pelt than a blanket, as if you had hunted Jünter and kept his skin and fur as a trophy. But all for the bargain price of €18.

NAME **WUSHOCK**

TEAM **WICHITA STATE UNIVERSITY**

SPORT **VARIOUS**

YEARS ACTIVE **1948–PRESENT**

STYLE **MUSCULAR WHEAT, WHICH YOU HAD NO IDEA WAS A THING UNTIL JUST NOW**

FAMOUS FOR **LOOKING LIKE AN EVEN ANGRIER DONALD TRUMP**

You'll be familiar with the movie trope of two very different lifeforms crossbreeding and giving rise to something altogether more frightening. Mostly this involves a human and some sort of scary animal with teeth or wings or claws. But in the case of Wichita State University's mascot, it's a human and some wheat. Sure.

Of course, it has some grounding in the fact that students at the university would, in days gone by, earn extra money in the fields harvesting such wheat, but it remains a maverick choice for a totem to spur on sports teams. If you think WuShock – named not because it's a New York rapper but a combination of the initials of Wichita University and 'Shockers', the name given to those wheat-gatherin' students – looks scary now, picture what it was like when it first came into existence. Back then it was just a head on a man otherwise wearing normal clothes, making it look rather too much like the disguise for a murderer than a mascot.

The back story is all well and good, but you can't really look past the elephant in the room. Or to be more specific, the giant muscular piece of wheat in the room, staring at you with bug eyes and clenched teeth like some sort of speed casualty who's spent the previous month in the gym. Whichever way you slice it, however accidental it was, with that hair . . . this guy is a ringer for Donald Trump.

NAME **SURI**

EVENT **COPA AMERICA**

SPORT **FOOTBALL**

YEAR ACTIVE **2011**

STYLE **IF THEY CAST AN OSTRICH IN THE LEAD OF *FEAR AND LOATHING IN LAS VEGAS***

FAMOUS FOR **CONTRIBUTIONS TO THE CHILD-THERAPY INDUSTRY**

Designing a mascot for an international tournament must feel like a bit of a free swing. They're only needed for a few weeks, nobody's really paying attention to them anyway and they'll be forgotten before you know it. Forgotten, that is, unless they end up haunting the nightmares of anyone who clapped eyes on them.

Suri is – was – apparently a rhea, which is a species of flightless bird, something of a relief because the only thing that could make it more unsettling would be if it could take to the skies and somehow swoop down on you and carry you away. Concocted for the 2011 Copa America, the best thing you can realistically say about it is that it was only around for a month or so.

Take your pick at which is the aspect most likely to make your kid cry. Is it the ludicrously long neck, giving off the strong vibes that someone tried to get sensitive information out of it by stretching the thing on a rack? Is it the bug eyes, which make it look like it's just rolled into Sin City with a bag full of mescaline? Maybe it's the thick eyebrows, nicked straight off the forehead of a Gallagher brother. Or maybe it's the whole package. God, take it away.

DANCE LIKE EVERYBODY'S WATCHING!

NAME **BARRY THE BODHRÁN**

EVENT **EUROPEAN UNDER-17S CHAMPIONSHIP**

SPORT **FOOTBALL**

YEAR ACTIVE **2019**

STYLE **AN ANTHROPOMORPHISED DRUM WITH THE EYES OF A DEMENTED TEDDY BEAR**

FAMOUS FOR **BEING PERHAPS THE ONLY EVER MASCOT DESIGNED TO HIT ITSELF IN THE FACE**

There was a time when nations, and the citizens of those nations, would do their absolute utmost to avoid stereotypes, hackneyed symbols and clichés about their country. Not now, apparently, for at the launch of the 2019 European Under-17s Championship, staged in Ireland, the mascot was unveiled as a human-sized bodhrán named Barry, with arms, legs, terrifying googly eyes and a cheeky little grin.

For those unfamiliar with the bodhrán, it's a handheld drum dating back to the 1700s and typically associated with traditional Celtic music; you can find cheap versions of the drum in any self-respecting Dublin tourist tat shop. It's a little like a tournament in England choosing a Union Jack-themed top hat as their mascot, or a giant cheeseburger for America.

We should say that Barry was designed by an 11-year-old schoolgirl, who was most likely delighted with the success of her choice. But adults, who should have by now got rid of the naivety of youth, approved this, and apparently didn't spot one of the biggest – but far from only – problem here: specifically, that any mascot whose main purpose is to hit itself in the face with a stick might not be an entirely wise choice.

NAME **STUFF THE MAGIC DRAGON**

TEAM **ORLANDO MAGIC**

SPORT **BASKETBALL**

YEARS ACTIVE **1988–PRESENT**

STYLE **WHAT WOULD HAPPEN IF YOU ASKED A FIVE-YEAR-OLD GIRL TO DESIGN A MASCOT**

FAMOUS FOR **ONCE PROPOSING TO KATE UPTON**

Toys for infants are designed to be as colourful as possible, to help advance as yet undeveloped minds. Perhaps that's what the Orlando Magic had in mind about sports fans when they came up with Stuff the Magic Dragon, a pun and a belch of every colour in a child's colouring set spread around a load of fur.

Stuff, with two stars on his head and two party-horn things that fire out of his nose in lieu of fire – as if to say, 'Yes, I am really a dragon, but I'm mainly here for fun!' – is known for larking around in the crowd, participating in the occasional slam dunk contest and once getting down on one knee to ask model Kate Upton to marry him a few years ago. Despite the logistical concerns about a human woman and a furry dragon consummating a marriage, she said yes at the time but sadly betrayed him by getting wed to baseball pitcher Justin Verlander.

This riot of gaudy colour is really the logical endpoint of the whole mascot concept: mascots are about treating everyone at a sporting event as if they're children, whether they are in fact children or not, so creating an 8ft-tall neon dragon is entirely fitting.

DANCE LIKE EVERYBODY'S WATCHING!

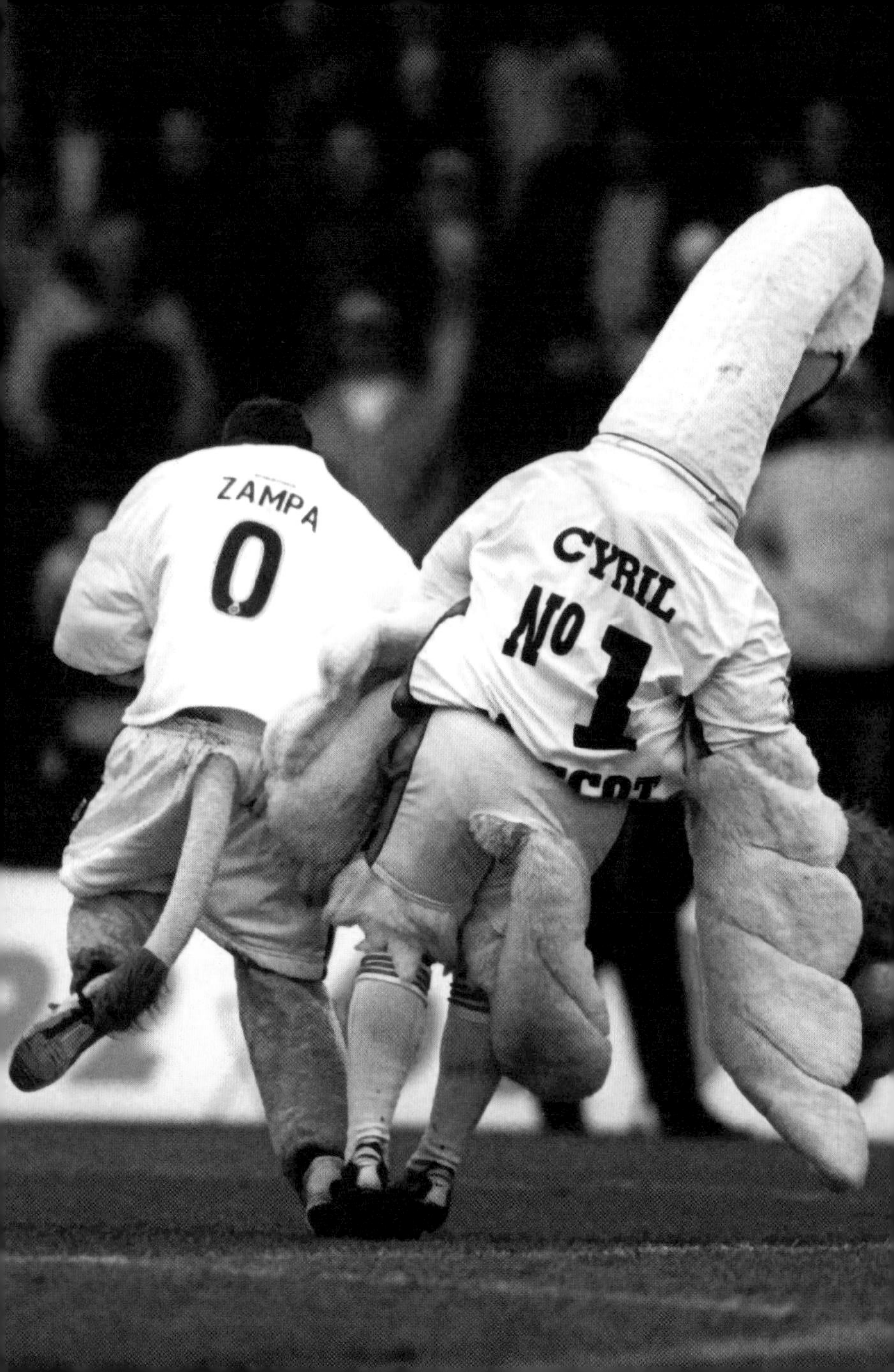
ZAMPA
0
CYRIL
No 1

WHEN MASCOTS ATTACK

A pig punching a wolf in the face. An elephant taking out an eagle with a bin. A duck and a cougar having to be separated by security. A bearcat being arrested for inciting a crowd to pelt an opposition player with snowballs.

If the possibility of seeing all that doesn't provide yet more evidence that watching sport is the best way to spend your time, then really you're probably taking life just a little bit too seriously. Because if there's one way to make the inherently pretty ridiculous concept of giant Muppets attempting to whip up an atmosphere even more ridiculous and entertaining, it's the sight of them wailing on each other.

Sometimes mascots get a bit too excited, and light-hearted japes turn physical. Take the infamous match between Bristol City and Wolves back in 1998, for example. It was the first game in charge for new Wolves manager Colin Lee, and striker David Connolly scored four in a 6–1 win having not found the net in 15 previous matches – but did anyone care about all of that? Clearly not. A giant wolf and a pig got into a fight on the pitch. Why would you remember the football after something as perfect as a wolf – who may or may not have blown their house down – fighting a pig?

Obviously, watching the thing is funny, as Wolfie the Wolverhampton Wanderers mascot and one of the Three Little Pigs – provided for the day by window installers Coldseal as a promotional stunt – face off in the centre circle, even if the filmed section of the fight was only a couple of punches thrown by both parties. But arguably even funnier than that are the statements given afterwards by the men inside the costumes.

'At half-time the wolf approached me and struck a blow to my head, which resulted in my head becoming detached from the pig body,' said Patrick Kelly, one of the pigs, presumably with a straight face. 'I then picked it up, retreated back to the Bristol half, followed by the wolf, which then again punched me.'

'I was defending the honour of my club,' solemnly responded Steve Bird, the man inside Wolfie, while at the same time expressing regret that Kelly had suffered a split lip.

Both clubs involved, as well as Coldseal Windows, put out statements as if they were dealing with a grave diplomatic incident, but ultimately no further action was taken, and the two combatants later kissed and made up on a TV chat show.

Still, at least those guys kept the violence between mascots. One of the more notorious mascots in recent footballing history was Swansea's Cyril the Swan, played for a number of years by a man named Eddie Donne. Cyril had already developed a reputation as a trouble-stirrer, managing to get himself banned from Norwich City, among other opposition clubs, by the time his team faced Millwall in 1998.

Cyril was going through his usual pre-match ritual of taunting the opposition fans, when the referee approached him before kick-off. 'All he said to me was, "Have I got to put up with this all game?"' Donne told ESPN. 'I nodded my head, and I butted him.'

Things went downhill from there. When Swansea went 3–0 up, Cyril could contain himself no longer. He ran onto the pitch and booted a ball into the face of a Millwall player, before rubbing the bald head of the linesman. The next time the two teams met, Millwall's mascot Zampa the Lion was out for revenge, and the two got into a genuine fist-fight, which ended with Cyril removing Zampa's head and drop-kicking it into the stands.

There had been a similar running feud during a college American football game between Coastal Carolina and James Madison universities in 2007. Duke Dog, the mascot for the latter, had apparently been taunting his opponent Chauncey the Chanticleer just a little too much, so a rumble ensued that started with a kick in the behind, continued to a vicious-looking spear tackle and ended with Duke reportedly saying, 'Don't tase me, bro,' as he was taken away by security. 'It really made people think about Duke Dog's character,' said a representative of the James Madison student body, as if he'd been caught drowning kittens.

There are plenty more such stories from college sports, where passions run high and the anonymity of the costume means people drop their inhibitions. Like the time Ohio University's Rufus Bobcat nailed Brutus from Ohio State; or the time the Oregon Duck was fired after attacking the Houston Cougar; or the time an innocent dance-off between Jawz the Jaguar and Eli the Eagle turned into a brawl.

And then, of course, occasionally even non-mascots get involved. NBA legend Charles Barkley was involved in a running feud with the Denver Nuggets mascot Rocky the Mountain Lion, which involved a number of initially playful but ultimately he-probably-actually-meant-it scraps. Rocky was even stopped in his tracks by a referee once, prevented from entering the court by a bop on the nose. And then there was the infamous time Sir Slapshot, the Atlanta Knights NHL team mascot, annoyed Cincinnati Cyclones coach Don Jackson one too many times, and Jackson climbed over a glass partition to show him what for.

So it's not all fun and games being a mascot. Sometimes, even if you're dressed up as a giant Muppet, you're not safe from the horrors of the world. But for the rest of us, the sight of two of these guys going at it will never, ever, not be funny.

NAME **MINAMO**

TEAM **FC GIFU, JAPAN**

SPORT **FOOTBALL**

YEARS ACTIVE **2014–PRESENT**

STYLE **LIFE-SIZE TROLL DOLL WEARING A BEANIE HAT**

FAMOUS FOR **BEING PERHAPS THE MOST HIGH-CONCEPT MASCOT IN THE WORLD**

FC Gifu, a Japanese football team, have a number of mascots. Their lead is Giffy, a curious character who frankly looks like the recent victim of a horrible crime, with something a little too similar to brain spilling out from the back of its head. Then there's Minamo, who's technically the mascot for the whole city and region, but can often be found with the football team anyway.

Looking a bit like a Troll doll wearing a circus big top-themed beanie hat, or perhaps like that evil kid from *The Invincibles* after dying his hair with some candy floss, Minamo might be the most high-concept, pretentious mascot of them all. Because *Minamo* basically translates as 'the water's surface', and this mascot is supposed to represent the 'sun glinting off the water's surface'. It sounds like it was thought up at 3am by some students who had been hitting the bongs pretty hard all day, and were getting, like, all deep.

Of course, the yellow is supposed to be the sun and the blue the clear blue streams, but come on, what is this? A yoga retreat? One of those shops that smells like soap and sells crystals? A stall at a festival where you can only buy hemp pants?

NAME **GEORGE THE GLORY GORILLA**

TEAM **PERTH GLORY**

SPORT **FOOTBALL**

YEARS ACTIVE **2011–PRESENT**

STYLE **PSYCHEDELIC SIMIAN WITH A PENCHANT FOR ANNOYING ANYONE HE SEES**

FAMOUS FOR **SIMULATING HEAVY URINATION USING A GRASS SPRINKLER**

In a country where football is some way down the list of national sporting priorities, you have to do something to grab the attention. And in the case of Perth Glory, they have decided that something is a purple gorilla. Notwithstanding that 'purple gorilla' sounds like a sordid euphemism, George the Glory Gorilla is a pretty intimidating prospect, with bright purple fur and an even brighter orange torso and face, looking like something you'd win by knocking some cans down at a fairground.

It doesn't help that he's constantly bearing his teeth, mouth stuck in a threatening rictus grin that's probably trying to say, 'Hey, kids, come join me and let's have some fun!' But it's actually saying 'Hey, kids, give me your candy floss or I'll rip your parents' arms off.'

George very much subscribes to the 'rambunctious' school of mascotting, his antics including picking up children, throwing them over his shoulder and taking them on their way (which, frankly, is frowned upon and could get him on a list somewhere), stealing food and drink from fans, on one memorable occasion straddling a sprinkler on the Glory pitch to make it look like the water was coming from, well, erm, his purple gorilla. And absolutely worst of all, the lowest of the low, entirely unforgivably, enthusiastically dancing to 'Gangnam Style'.

NAME **STOLLE**

TEAM **HOLSTEIN KIEL**

SPORT **FOOTBALL**

YEARS ACTIVE **2007–PRESENT**

STYLE **GAWKY 9FT-TALL STORK WEARING ITS DAD'S SHIRT**

FAMOUS FOR **BEING AVAILABLE FOR KIDS' PARTIES AT A REASONABLE HOURLY RATE**

Modern life is full of contradictions. Rarely are things black and white. Every animal, mineral or vegetable has conflicting elements. So in many ways Stolle, a 9ft stork who represents German football team Holsten Kiel, might be the most perfect mascot to represent these troubled times. Take the Q&A he did for the club website, in which he was asked what he liked to eat. 'I prefer to eat frogs and enemies,' he said, chillingly, presumably while staring the interviewer directly in the eyes and drawing his wing across his neck. Whereas, later on, he listed among his hobbies 'being cuddled and making people laugh'.

The message? Sure, I am a mascot, and thus enjoy a snuggle and of course some light comedy, but do not cross me, for I will devour you.

But the good news is that, if you have the time, inclination, money and desire to harm your offspring for life, you can hire Stolle for a very reasonable rate: just €100 (plus VAT) an hour, in fact, for this giant, lanky stork – who for some reason wears a shirt at least three sizes too big – to provide entertainment at your next function. Where, presumably, he'll either hug you or swallow you whole.

NAME **STANFORD TREE**

TEAM **STANFORD UNIVERSITY MARCHING BAND**

SPORT **NONE AS SUCH**

YEARS ACTIVE **1975–PRESENT**

STYLE **WELL, IT'S A TREE. A TREE. NOT SURE WHAT ELSE TO SAY**

FAMOUS FOR **BEING CAUTIONED BY POLICE FOR BEING DRUNK AT A BASKETBALL GAME**

Technically the mascot of the Stanford University marching band rather than a specific team, the Stanford Tree is an ever-evolving being that regenerates every couple of years – like a sort of Doctor Who, but instead of an ageless time lord it's an anthropomorphic tree in various guises, each designed to be more unsettling than the last.

The version most likely to feature in therapy sessions in years to come is a bug-eyed effort that looks half the result of a last-minute art project thrown together in a panic with whatever scraps of material were lying around, half a drugs casualty on day three of a festival. Imagine seeing this thing out and about after about 9pm – it must be the most pepper-sprayed mascot in America.

Because the Tree is usually 'played' by students, various alcohol-related incidents have occurred over the years, including the memorable occasion when the Tree was spotted swigging booze from a hip flask during a basketball game and was giving a ticking off by the local police. 'The tree's movement is usually consistent with that of someone who's had something to drink,' a university spokesperson solemnly explained after the incident.

NAME **MYSTERIOUS FISH**

TEAM **CHIBA LOTTE MARINES**

SPORT **BASEBALL**

YEARS ACTIVE **2017–PRESENT**

STYLE **NEON ANGELFISH WITH A HUMANOID BODY**

FAMOUS FOR **VOMITING ITS OWN SKELETON THROUGH ITS MOUTH**

It won't be news to you that baseball is huge in Japan. Combine that love for the game with a stereotypical fascination with bright lights and colours, and you get this unnamed mascot – simply referred to as the 'Mysterious Fish' on their website – for the Chiba Lotte Marines Japanese baseball team. It's a creature that is ostensibly a garish angelfish (a pretty nightmarish thing with dead eyes and sharp teeth in its own right) with a bright blue head, who runs around the field, sometimes sparring with other mascots, sometimes whipping the crowd into a frenzy, but sometimes doing something rather more troubling.

You see, this guy's party piece is for the person in the suit to wriggle their body through the gaping mouth of the fish, leap out and then thrash around on the floor like . . . well . . . like a fish out of water. They wear a skeleton suit within the broader fish suit, bones painted on their back and fish skull atop their head with its own wide, mirthlessly grinning mouth. All of which means this family friendly mascot is essentially puking its own spine out, then leaving its now decapitated head rolling around on the floor, like some sort of appalling cross between *Game of Thrones* and Hello Kitty. What fun for all the family! Two mascots in one, the second more horrifying than the first!

NAME **BIG RED**

TEAM **WESTERN KENTUCKY UNIVERSITY**

SPORT **BASKETBALL**

YEARS ACTIVE **1979–PRESENT**

STYLE **RED. BIG. RED AND BIG. BIG AND RED. RED AND RED. BIG AND BIG. BIG. RED.**

FAMOUS FOR **UNSUCCESSFULLY SUING SILVIO BERLUSCONI (SORT OF)**

What is Big Red? He looks like he could be a big red frog . . . but isn't. He looks like he could be a sort of very twisted version of a bright red human . . . but isn't. Actually, he isn't really a he. The Big Red Manifesto declared that Big Red must always be red, must always have the college's initials stamped on its front, is neither male nor female and cannot talk. Big Red is nothing and everything. Big Red is nobody and he is all of us. Big Red cannot be pigeonholed or defined, and will not live by your rules.

Or Big Red could just be a large blob and a bit of fun, something into which too many deep things should not be read. Big Red is weird, though, a sort of large teddy bear thing with a massive mouth into which various things and sometimes people are shovelled. But perhaps the really interesting thing about Big Red came when the university took Italian media company Mediaset, owned by former Prime Minister Silvio Berlusconi, to court over a copyright claim.

Some 12 years after Big Red's arrival on the scene, a character called Gabibbo appeared on Italian TV, bearing a very striking resemblance to Big Red. Suspicions were further raised when Gabibbo's creator admitted the design came to him after seeing a picture of Big Red, leading to the university suing Mediaset for $250 million. Brilliantly, Big Red travelled to Italy for the hearing in 2004, even giving an impromptu press conference. Alas, the suit was unsuccessful.

NAME **BOILER MAN**

TEAM **WEST BROMWICH ALBION**

SPORT **FOOTBALL**

YEARS ACTIVE **2018–PRESENT**

STYLE **A CHILDREN'S ENTERTAINER, BUT IN THE SHAPE OF A STANDARD COMBI BOILER**

FAMOUS FOR **BEING PERHAPS THE FIRST SPORTS MASCOT TO BE STYLED AFTER AN ITEM USED FOR HOUSEHOLD HEATING**

A tie-in with shirt sponsors Ideal Boilers, Boiler Man showed up on the touchline for West Brom's first game of the 2018/19 season in what most people had assumed would be a short-lived gimmick. But he's stuck around, larking about with the kids before games, mugging for the camera and almost making you forget for a few minutes that this is a bloke dressed as a boiler strutting around the pitch and resignedly accepting the chain of events that led to this point for humanity.

Boiler Man seems here to stay, too. He has an active social media presence, has featured in several adverts (in one he appears to seduce a middle-aged lady in a jacuzzi. Seriously) and launched a range of merchandise. If you have spare cash lying around that you actively want to waste, you can buy a Boiler Man baseball cap, a Boiler Man mug, a Boiler Man air freshener or a T-shirt that bears the legend 'MY IDEAL MAN IS BOILER MAN'.

This is all very well, but it's Baggie Bird we feel sorry for. Stalwart of the touchline and official West Brom mascot, Baggie has been relegated to the shadows a little, still doing its best to keep the crowd entertained but knowing all the while people are simply saying, 'Hang on . . . is that a boiler?'

NAME SEBASTIAN THE IBIS

TEAM **UNIVERSITY OF MIAMI**

SPORT **AMERICAN FOOTBALL**

YEARS ACTIVE **1957–PRESENT**

STYLE **EXTREMELY ANGRY, FOR WHAT BASICALLY LOOKS LIKE A DUCK**

FAMOUS FOR **INVADING THE STAGE AND DANCING ON JIMMY FALLON'S *TONIGHT SHOW***

The ibis – a wading bird with a long beak to pluck fish from the water – is a rather elegant animal, sort of a mini, understated flamingo. But if the ibis has lawyers, they might want to get in touch with the people that designed the costume for Sebastian, the mascot of the University of Miami, because they'd have a good case for some serious misrepresentation.

Sebastian, rather than the graceful bird of reality, looks more like a cross between Donald Duck and the Joker, a nefarious character with an evil grin and the eyes of someone who is about to steal an old lady's life savings and enjoy watching her cry. Apparently the ibis is known as a brave bird, one that will save other birds when hurricanes approach, which was the reason why the university adopted it as one of their symbols way back in 1926. But this guy looks like he'd shove whatever bird came near him in the way of any passing hurricane – maybe not even to save himself, just for sport.

Sebastian engages in the usual sort of mascot japes, but with that twisted grin and those unfeeling, vicious eyes, it all takes on a rather different tone to the loveable high jinks of your standard cuddly sort. If you want a sidekick to a Bond villain, give Sebastian a call. But if you want to entertain some kids in a light-hearted way, ask anyone else.

NAME **BURNIE**

TEAM **MIAMI HEAT**

SPORT **BASKETBALL**

YEARS ACTIVE **1988–PRESENT**

STYLE **A FIREBALL BROUGHT TO LIFE**

FAMOUS FOR **BEING THE SUBJECT OF MULTIPLE LAWSUITS**

We all understand that mascots are supposed to be anarchic and have a little fun. And hey, you know, sometimes that fun will just nudge over the line – take that, squares. The problem with Burnie, the mascot of the Miami Heat – Geddit?! Burnie! Heat! – is that he has sprinted past the line and, appropriately enough, set fire to the line on multiple occasions, to the point where you wonder why they bother with him.

Burnie, a version of the Heat's fireball logo brought to life, but with half a basketball for a nose, has been the subject of at least three lawsuits down the years that can all be put down to, shall we say, excessive boisterousness. There was the security guard in 2018 who claimed she injured her leg after being barged by Burnie. There was the teacher who wasn't impressed when Burnie got a little carried away during a dance routine during a visit to her school, lifted up her leg and allegedly tore her hip.

And then, all the way back in 1994 during a game in Puerto Rico, Burnie dragged a woman from the crowd and engaged in some enthusiastic dancing, seemingly against her will, and she fell. Unluckily for Burnie, the woman turned out to be the wife of a local judge, and sued the Heat for $1 million for assault and emotional distress. The Heat offered $100,000, but in the end the court awarded only $50,000. Everyone gets a little giddy, but it doesn't always cost that much money.

NAMES **GOLEO VI AND PILLE**

EVENT **WORLD CUP**

SPORT **FOOTBALL**

YEAR ACTIVE **2006**

STYLE **A LION WHO WORE A T-SHIRT BUT NOTHING ELSE, AND A TALKING FOOTBALL**

FAMOUS FOR **BEING TERRIFYING IN VARIOUS DIFFERENT WAYS**

Take a look at that picture. What animal would you say that is? A camel in disguise? A deformed house cat? A lion? You might get there after a few guesses, but it genuinely isn't obvious what this guy is supposed to be. And what's that he's holding in his hand? Why, it's a talking football, just the sort of thing to definitely not give nightmares to anyone who encounters it.

Still, despite being an inanimate object with a mouth and a lion that doesn't look anything like a lion, they went down very well with football's top brass. 'Goleo VI is a great guy and he looks fantastic. Even his name tells you he's a big football fan!' enthused Franz Beckenbauer. 'Goleo VI has a lot of self-confidence. Still, he's not quite Brazilian with a football! But as a mascot, he's certainly in a class of his own,' was Pele's verdict. They were both sincere opinions held by these two grand old men of the world game, words they absolutely, 100 per cent, definitely thought up and said themselves, on their own, with nobody else prompting them.

But here's the central problem with Goleo. He's wearing a T-shirt. It's a plain white T-shirt with 06 on it: nothing to get worked up about there. He's also wearing boots, which does raise the question of what he's kicking: is it his mate Pille, the talking football? Seems just a little harsh to have a conversation with something, then boot it in the face. But that's all he's wearing. T-shirt . . . boots . . . but no pants. We wouldn't be surprised if Goleo finds himself in trouble in a park late at night with that get-up.

NAME **SPARKY THE SUN DEVIL**

TEAM **ARIZONA STATE UNIVERSITY**

SPORT **AMERICAN FOOTBALL**

YEARS ACTIVE **1951–PRESENT**

STYLE **WALT DISNEY, BUT ON FIRE**

FAMOUS FOR **CRUSHING BUSES**

Arizona State University simply cannot make up their minds, mascot-wise. It's been an owl, a bulldog, and naturally, obviously, in the clear progression of things, it's now a sun devil. In 1946 the university wanted to refresh its image a little, to make it more distinct and reflect the climate of Tempe, Arizona. That climate being . . . hotter than the sun. Thus, Sparky the Sun Devil was born, designed by a former Disney animator called Bert Anthony. The visual similarity between Sparky and Walt Disney is not, you would assume, coincidental.

While you can only speculate on why a former employee of Walt Disney chose to model a mascot on him that is quite literally a devil, these days Sparky looks a bit more like either a gentleman thief, twizzling his moustache diabolically as he makes off with yet another heiress's pearls, or someone who has taken some spray paint to one of those *V for Vendetta* masks.

In addition to his flawless facial hair, there's a slightly curious Sparky tradition, in which he's depicted in a film as arriving on earth from the very heart of the sun, striding across the Arizona desert and arriving at the university, stomping on the bus of the visiting team on the way. Sort of like the Stay Puft Marshmallow Man from *Ghostbusters*, only more . . . flamey.

NAME **COZMO**

TEAM **LA GALAXY**

SPORT **FOOTBALL**

YEARS ACTIVE **2001–PRESENT**

STYLE **AN ALIEN WHOSE HEART'S DESIRE IS TO PLAY SOCCER**

FAMOUS FOR **TROLLING JOSÉ MOURINHO BEFORE A PRE-SEASON FRIENDLY**

The LA Galaxy's mascot used to be terrible. In the team's early days he was a character called Twizzle, who was essentially just a spaceman running around the field and not really being much use to anyone. They then brought in Cozmo, who was initially a slightly gormless green character, who looked like a cartoon baby dinosaur.

But having realised that everyone looks cooler wearing black, Cozmo's colour was changed to the mascot we know and love today. He still looks a bit vacant, still has eyebrows that Carlo Ancelotti would be proud of, and still occasionally wears one of those stupid hats with the mini propeller on the top, but after some significant trial and error the Galaxy settled on his present form. A few years ago Cozmo did a parachute jump into their home stadium, and before a pre-season friendly he greeted José Mourinho, everyone's favourite friendly manager, with a big banner that simply read: 'It's Called Soccer'. And he's right. It is.

Usually the blurb about these mascots is pretty toe-curling, filled with corporate-speak that is theoretically supposed to be cool but, as with everything that is supposed to be cool, is nothing like cool. But you have to take your hat off to this line in Cozmo's bio on the Galaxy website: 'Cozmo wanted to try out for the team but due to unforeseen circumstances (he is not human) he was not allowed to play in MLS.'

DANCE LIKE EVERYBODY'S WATCHING!

GARETH EVANS
AKA HARRY THE HORNET

Watford's Harry the Hornet is among the most notorious mascots in English football, having come to prominence after landing in the middle of an argument between his club and rivals Crystal Palace. Gareth Evans has played Harry since 2008, despite having had very little intention of being a mascot at the start . . .

Harry the Hornet has been going for quite a long time, but you've been Harry since 2008. How did you start out?

It was a running joke to start with, really. My understanding at the time was Watford Football Club were looking for someone to be Harry consistently, rather than having a different person every time. There was no real love for the character; people would wear it for one game, wave to the crowd, then someone else would do it at the next game. I heard that they were after someone to do it more permanently and so I said, 'Yeah, I'll do it.' I was only having a laugh, mind – I really just wanted to see what their reaction would be. After a few weeks the club said, 'We've put your name down.' I said, 'What? No, I was joking!' But true to my word, I did it.

The first game was a bit weird, a bit surreal, but by the second or third game I grew into it. I thought, if I'm going to do this, let's do it properly. Let's not be a normal, standard mascot. Let's give it a character. Let's let it grow. And we have what we have today, which is probably the No.1 mascot in the country. Not my words . . . [Harry is regularly ranked as among the best mascots in the Premier League].

Were you given any instructions about what to do by Watford? Did they tell you what to do, and what not to do?

They just said, 'Enjoy yourself, get out there, get the crowd going.' I knew the dos and don'ts – pretty much common sense, really. Even today I don't plan anything. In the latter part of my first season I found a drum in a locker and just thought, 'I'm having that.' Didn't ask anybody, brought it to the edge of the pitch and started banging it. The fans joined in, the players responded – job done. Suddenly Harry had a drum!

I used to dance when I was a kid, so I brought that into the personality, into the act. I used to practise the night before every game at home, until my partner moved in. It's a lot of hard work and commitment. Every other Saturday you're kind of getting ready to get into a different headspace, to be someone else.

Have you ever got into trouble with the club?

There have been no real areas where I've been told off, but I have been told, 'That's close to the mark . . .' If we score a goal and I run on the pitch, I know that would be breaking the rules – so I don't do it. I'm trusted to be on the sidelines next to the pitch. Harry is an integral part of the club, with our community vibe that we have. He's the link between the fans and the club, so I'm very fortunate. I take heart that I've grown a character that is much loved – and not just by Watford supporters.

You've been a Watford fan since you were a kid. Does being Harry change how you are as a fan?

I put so much effort into being Harry that I forget I'm actually a fan. I jump and cheer, but in the costume it's a very different experience. When I'm Harry, it's very difficult to tell what's going on in the game. I do look forward to going back to being a fan at Vicarage Road, but I'll certainly miss the buzz, no pun intended. Hopefully that's in years to come – I've plenty more to give.

If results are bad, you can't sulk. I did sulk once and I got a bollocking for it, and rightfully so, because you've got to be there to lift everyone up. One year [2013] we were going for automatic promotion but ended up getting pushed into the play-offs, where we lost to Leeds on the very last day. In our minds – after a superb season – we were all thinking, 'Promotion, promotion, promotion,' then we lost and I was gutted. And knackered. That was the fan in me, and everyone could tell. I was lying on the floor and everyone was like, 'Gareth, you shouldn't be like that.'

You've even put your body on the line to be Harry . . .

I was doing a charity game, and we were having a half-time penalty shoot-out. The pitch was soaking and when I took one I tried to just put a little bit of spin on it, but my legs went up in the air. I came

DANCE LIKE EVERYBODY'S WATCHING!

down on my arm and it just broke in half. Eight weeks in a cast, completely broken elbow.

Fortunately it was at the end of the season so I had the summer to recuperate. It's something to laugh about now . . . but not at the time. The pain . . . I can't describe. I picked myself up, went straight down the tunnel, took off the costume and went straight to hospital. The hospital got me turned around in 45 minutes into a temporary cast, and I was back in time for the post-match meal.

You and Harry got quite a lot of attention after a game when some fans accused Crystal Palace's Wilfried Zaha of diving, and you had a bit of fun with him. It was all over the papers that you pretended to dive at his feet.

First and foremost, I dived about six metres behind him, not at his feet. In all honesty, I didn't really know what had gone on. I heard it from some fans. Zaha is a fantastic footballer, no doubt about it. He's gone past me as he's walking down the tunnel, the fans are calling him a diver, so I've just dived on the ground. Nothing more, nothing less. I've walked away and got a reaction from the Palace fans, so I did it again. Why wouldn't I?

I had no idea what was going to play out. It was my friend's birthday that night, so I went out. I was watching *Match of the Day* in the pub, and they zoomed in on Harry. I was laughing, Alan Shearer was laughing, Ian Wright was laughing – they were all laughing.

But some people took it a bit more seriously . . .

I didn't understand what would happen the next day, with all these newspapers saying I'd dived at his feet. I contacted someone at the club saying I hadn't, and they said, 'We know.' I sent a message to [Watford striker] Troy Deeney and said, 'You scored your 100th goal for the club and I'm getting the attention – I'm so sorry.'

My life certainly changed a little bit after that: social media lockdown, Instagram private. Some journalists called me; I said, 'No comment,' and they respected it. But I opened up one of the papers the next day and there were pictures from my Facebook, naming where I worked – that was difficult to take. It was worrying, because then you think: what is going to be posted about me, my private

life, etcetera? That's very daunting because I'm not in the public eye. Usually people are reacting to Harry, but now they were reacting to Gareth Evans – and that's quite difficult.

It was brought up a few times, and Sam Allardyce, who was Crystal Palace manager at the time, and Roy Hodgson who took over from him, both reacted.

I felt sorry for Sam Allardyce because he didn't see it. He would have just been told that the mascot dived. And then it rolled onto Roy Hodgson. A journalist said to him, completely out of the blue, 'What about Watford's mascot?' Hodgson's response [he called Harry 'disgraceful'] was correct; if I had thrown myself at a professional footballer's feet, I would deserve to be banned. But I didn't do that. The whole thing got totally blown out of proportion. Now everyone was looking at Zaha diving since that episode . . .

DANCE LIKE EVERYBODY'S WATCHING!

. . . but he actually reacted pretty well. He tweeted you a picture of some diving judges giving scores out of ten, and you responded in kind, and that was all very good humoured.

It probably took a bit of time for Wilf to process what had happened because a man in a giant hornet costume had kind of shown him up – or his reaction did. He tweeted, I responded, then that gets seen 250,000 times. I had support from the club because they knew I had done nothing wrong versus the media circus.

I learned a long time ago that when you put something on social media, it's then not yours. That time it really hit home. But I've kept the newspaper clippings.

NAME **DONNY DOG**

TEAM **DONCASTER ROVERS**

SPORT **FOOTBALL**

YEARS ACTIVE **1999–PRESENT**

STYLE **LOVEABLE HOUND WHO WOULDN'T LOOK OUT OF PLACE ON A SATURDAY MORNING KIDS' TV SHOW**

FAMOUS FOR **MOONLIGHTING AS A GLAMOUR MODEL**

Aside from looking a bit like the dog van from *Dumb and Dumber*, Donny Dog is probably exactly the sort of thing you'd picture if you had to visualise a relatively low-key sporting mascot. Nice, friendly, inoffensive, will wave and lollop around, good to keep the youngsters occupied and – crucially – won't cause the club too many problems.

Hmmm. Yes. About that last bit. A few years ago Donny was played by a woman named Tracy Chandler, who was offered the chance to raise a bit of money for charity by posing for some shots for the *Sunday Sport*, a publication known for featuring ladies in as few items of clothing as possible. Chandler was not wearing the Donny costume in the photos, but she wasn't wearing a great deal else either. This wasn't at all well received at Doncaster, and Chandler was dismissed from her position.

However, after something of a backlash from the fans, sensible heads ultimately prevailed – it was for charity, after all, plus the photos were pretty tame, featuring Chandler in her underwear but nothing more top shelf, so it was a bit unclear who exactly she was harming. Chairman John Ryan eventually changed his mind, declared the whole thing to be one big misunderstanding and restored Chandler to her role, which she continued to play for several more years.

NAME **MAD ANT**

TEAM FORT WAYNE MAD ANTS

SPORT BASKETBALL

YEARS ACTIVE 2007–PRESENT

STYLE LIKE THE FLY, BUT SUB AN ANT AND CONOR MCGREGOR FOR A FLY AND JEFF GOLDBLUM

FAMOUS FOR BEING THE ONLY ANT THAT COULD PUT YOU IN A HEADLOCK AND STEAL YOUR LUNCH MONEY

Older readers will be familiar with *The Fly*, a 1986 film in which Jeff Goldblum plays an eccentric scientist who ends up being genetically fused with a fly, so that he becomes a fly–human hybrid monster that gradually becomes less of the latter and more of the former. That must be what happened when the Fort Wayne Mad Ants were thinking up a mascot, with the muscles of an MMA fighter joined together with, well, an ant. It's the sort of mascot that is just as likely to pick you up and twirl you round its head as it is to perform low-key antics before a basketball game.

For the first few years of his life the Mad Ant was even more terrifying than the simple concept behind him; which, as the concept is a 6ft ant who looks like he has spent three years eating creatine and lifting dumbbells, is quite a feat. He was initially red and yellow, with the maniacal grin of an action-movie villain who's about to run through a 32nd-floor window and antennae that looked disconcertingly lifelike.

But now, after the team adopted the colours of its parent club, the Indiana Pacers, he's now a little more subdued, his navy blue and yellow simply making him unsettling rather than a genuine threat to your soul. 'He's a little softer and a little less muscular,' a team suit said. 'And now he's blue instead of red. He's supposed to appeal to young children.' May those children one day recover.

NAME **BLUE BLOB**

TEAM **XAVIER UNIVERSITY**

SPORT **BASKETBALL**

YEARS ACTIVE **1985–PRESENT**

STYLE **THE COOKIE MONSTER, IF HE HAD BEEN LEFT IN THE SUN FOR TOO LONG**

FAMOUS FOR **HIS SIGNATURE MOVE, WHICH IS . . . ROLLING. ROLLING LIKE A BLOB**

Ever since 1925, the sports teams of Xavier University in Cincinnati, Ohio, have been known as the Musketeers, and as such for a long time their sole mascot was D'Artagnan, a fellow with the appropriate pointy facial hair and weirdly big muscles who swashed and buckled before, during and after games. Trouble was, D'Artagnan seemed a bit cold, a bit threatening, a bit of an old timer and quite possibly a bit too goateed. No kid likes that. Especially the goatee bit.

So in order to be a little more cuddly, a little more fun, they brought in someone else. Or something else. How exactly do you address a blob? Anyway, not wishing to complicate things they called the blue blob they'd created 'Blue Blob', something that sort of resembles a mop dipped in blue paint, or the Cookie Monster if you left him out in the sun and he started melting.

The Blob and D'Artagnan often form a duo, the latter taking the role of the preening, flexing jock, while the Blob's signature move is to simply roll around the basketball court when his adoring public demands that he rolls. You can overcomplicate many things in life, not least the mascot game, so it feels quite nice that this mascot is just a ball of blue fur that occasionally rolls around. Less is more.

NAME KINGSLEY

TEAM PARTICK THISTLE

SPORT FOOTBALL

YEARS ACTIVE 2015—PRESENT

STYLE FRIGHTENING THE LIVING DAYLIGHTS OUT OF THE WHOLE CROWD

FAMOUS FOR THE ONLY MASCOT TO HAVE EARNED A MONOGRAPH FROM THE GUARDIAN'S ART CRITIC JONATHAN JONES

Created by Turner Prize-shortlisted Scottish artist David Shrigley, Kingsley landed on Partick Thistle's touchlines in 2015, replacing the hitherto popular Jaggee MacBee and Pee Tee the Toucan. And let's just say the reaction was not entirely positive, which you might not be that surprised about, considering that Kingsley looks somewhere between – as Irvine Welsh noted – Lisa Simpson after a six-month meth binge and the sun reacting with horror as it explodes.

'He represents the angst of being a football fan,' explained Shrigley, 'which anyone who has supported Partick Thistle over the last few decades understands. People are saying: "He's terrible, he's a disgrace to the good name of mascots." Do mascots have a good name? Do they have a union? If you look on the internet, as I did yesterday, you can find a far scarier mascot.'

Well, that latter point is true, at least. Named after the Partick sponsor at the time, Kingsford Capital Management, Kingsley was the first and only mascot to receive an appraisal from the art pages of the *Guardian*. Jonathan Jones, the paper's art critic, compared Kingsley to the art of the Spanish surrealist Joan Miró, said it was 'a roaring manifestation of soccer's energy' and quoted Oscar Wilde recalling 'the rage of Caliban at seeing his own face in the glass'. It's, erm, just a mascot, JJ.

NAME **SQUATCH**

TEAM **SEATTLE SUPERSONICS**

SPORT **BASKETBALL**

YEARS ACTIVE **1993–2008**

STYLE **CHEWBACCA'S MORE CHEERFUL COUSIN**

FAMOUS FOR **TRYING TO SET A WORLD RECORD FOR JUMPING OVER CARS IN INLINE SKATES, AND FAILING**

What's one thing everyone knows about basketball players? They're tall! What's one thing that everyone knows is tall and is also associated with the Seattle area? Sasquatch! When you think of it like that, the choice of mascot for the Seattle Supersonics NBA team makes perfect sense. And thus, Squatch was born, Seattle's answer to Chewbacca, although Squatch is probably less likely to pull your arms off if he loses. But you wouldn't rule it out.

Squatch was something of a daredevil, and for reasons that aren't entirely clear tried to demonstrate this by attempting to set a world record by jumping 30 feet over some cars owned by two Supersonics players, wearing inline skates. Sadly, he was unsuccessful, clearing the cars but failing to reach 30 feet. As a consolation, Squatch is also one of the few mascots to have a song written in his honour by a rock star, after Chris Bellew, singer in the band The Presidents of the USA, wrote 'S.Q.U.A.T.C.H' in 2007. In 2008, however, the Supersonics relocated to the decidedly less 'big footy' area of Oklahoma City, and Squatch was retired.

In some ways having a mythical creature like this as a sporting mascot is extremely fitting, because if there's one thing that believers in things like the Sasquatch and sports fans have in common it's a basic optimism that frequently has absolutely no grounding in fact. In the same way people think their team is going to win, people think mysterious 8ft apes who roam around wooded areas are real. We're all part of the same mindset, like it or not.

NAME **THE CITY GENT**

TEAM **BRADFORD CITY**

SPORT **FOOTBALL**

YEARS ACTIVE **c.1960s–2013**

STYLE **A MAN IN A BOWLER HAT CARRYING A BRIEFCASE**

FAMOUS FOR **BEING SACKED AFTER 'LOSING TOO MUCH WEIGHT'**

Most of the mascots in this book have a costume of some description, something at least to shield the face of the human being within. Not the City Gent, Bradford City's mascot from the 1960s until relatively recently, however. Based on a cartoon of a former chairman, the City Gent was, of course, a man wearing a Bradford kit, complemented perfectly by the natural accessories one would expect – a bowler hat, a large umbrella and a briefcase. Why? What did you think he was going to wear?

For nearly 20 years the Gent, a portly character who would parade up and down the pitch whipping up the home fans and aggravating those of City's opponents, was played by a man called Lenny Berry, but in 2013 it was reported that Bradford had dismissed him after he lost too much weight when he was diagnosed with diabetes, thus no longer fitting the profile of the Gent. But there had been complaints about Berry's 'behaviour, demeanour and attitude', including reports of some of the fruity language he was alleged to have used, from a couple of clubs, so the weight thing appears to have merely been a smokescreen to edge him out.

It's things like this that make you realise that sport, or at least how seriously we take it all, is ultimately very silly indeed. 'We feel the way the story's been told on his side has breached confidentiality and forced us to reveal more details of the story,' a Bradford official solemnly intoned when the weight controversy emerged, with nobody apparently pausing to consider that they were dealing with a middle-aged man who wore formal shoes with a football kit, not intricate debates about the state of the economy.

DANCE LIKE EVERYBODY'S WATCHING!

NAME **RAYMOND**

TEAM **TAMPA BAY RAYS**

SPORT **BASEBALL**

YEARS ACTIVE **1998—PRESENT**

STYLE **A HAIRY OLD MAN WITH DONALD TRUMP'S SPARE WIG**

FAMOUS FOR **HAVING TO APOLOGISE FOR AN OFF-COLOUR JOKE ABOUT STEVE IRWIN**

Mascots are supposed to be a lot of things. They're supposed to be cute. They're supposed to be loveable. They're supposed to be entertaining. They are not – repeat, not – supposed to be edgy. So it's no wonder that the Tampa Bay Rays had to apologise in 2013 when Raymond, their furry, cuddly, loveable mascot, held up a sign handed to him by a fan that said 'Rays to do list: 1) Steve Irwin, 2) World Series', with Irwin's name crossed out. If you weren't aware, Irwin was the Australian wildlife expert and TV personality who was killed by a stingray in 2006. Ooof.

When he's not needlessly offending people with jokes about the dead, Raymond is . . . well, we're not really sure what Raymond is. He sort of looks like the Phillie Phanatic, if you left him in a cupboard for about three years so his fur faded and he got some sort of weird gunk all over him, and then patched him up with odds and ends of fabric from an off-cuts box. On his head is what appears to be one of Donald Trump's spare hairpieces, while over his nose and ears are bits of floppy fringey stuff that look like they have been stolen from the bottom of an old lady's sofa.

The problem with Raymond is . . . he's just a bit dull. Even the name, while making sense from a practical point of view, doesn't exactly give the impression he's going to whip a crowd into a frenzy. Raymond will do your taxes, Raymond will trim your hedge, Raymond will always have a set of powertools you can borrow. But lead a stadium in song? Nah. Maybe that's why he tried to be edgy . . .

DANCE LIKE EVERYBODY'S WATCHING!

NAME **RAPIDMAN**

TEAM **COLORADO RAPIDS**

SPORT **FOOTBALL**

YEARS ACTIVE **1996–2007**

STYLE **JOHNNY BRAVO FUSED WITH BART SIMPSON FUSED WITH A SMURF**

FAMOUS FOR **BEING GRANTED A TESTIMONIAL MATCH**

What is it with mascots in the US having to look jacked, like they spend half their time in the gym and the other half injecting pure protein into their veins? Combine that with teeth that could blind passing pigeons, the wrap-around shades of someone's dad who thinks they're the hippest cat in town, blue skin and Bart Simpson's hair, and you've got RapidMan, the former mascot of the Colorado Rapids MLS side.

Now retired, presumably to spend more time with the rest of the Smurfs, RapidMan was billed as the ultimate cool dude, as marketing executives across America tried desperately to make this strange new sport 'soccer' a going concern in a country already quite well stacked for sports.

RapidMan was basically the 1990s in mascot form: almost certainly the only reason he didn't wear a Global Hypercolor T-shirt was that he sort of had to wear the team jersey. It's no wonder they eventually decided to move him on, and in 2007 RapidMan was replaced by a rotating roster of mascots including half-pun, half-buffalo Marco Van Bison, Edson the Eagle and Jorge el Mapache, a giant racoon goalkeeper. But not before RapidMan had been awarded a testimonial game to help him in retirement.

NAMES **MOONBEAM AND MOONCHESTER**

TEAM MANCHESTER CITY

SPORT FOOTBALL

YEARS ACTIVE 1996–PRESENT

STYLE PERPETUALLY SMILING, POTENTIALLY DERANGED

FAMOUS FOR TRAVELLING FROM OUTER SPACE IN THE MID-1990s TO SUPPORT MANCHESTER CITY, FOR SOME REASON

Once upon a time, Manchester was famous for its nightlife, with clubs like the Hacienda providing a fertile ground for house music and young scallywags to get up to all sorts. Some of them, whisper it quietly, would occasionally dabble in the odd naughty nocturnal livener, the sort that might make one's facial features artificially light up for the whole evening. Still, we're sure it's just a coincidence that Manchester City's first mascot had colossal fixed smile and pupils you could drive a truck through.

Derived from the City anthem 'Blue Moon', Moonchester arrived at the start of the 1996 season, supposedly from the actual moon, although it was never convincingly explained why an alien who had just infiltrated the human race would choose to eschew building relationships between species or exploring this new world in favour of rocking up at a football club that had just been relegated from the Premier League.

A few years later – with Moonchester apparently having become very lonely – a partner arrived from beyond the earth's atmosphere, displaying a similarly manic smile and the same black-hole pupils (albeit square, like 'her' sweetheart's). Moonbeam and Moonchester were truly meant to be together. Still, they might have had the last laugh: perhaps their alien superpower was to look into the future and predict the arrival of money and otherworldly football to City.

NAME **SCREECH**

TEAM **WASHINGTON NATIONALS**

SPORT **BASEBALL**

YEARS ACTIVE **2005–PRESENT**

STYLE **A BALD EAGLE, NOT THE CHARACTER FROM**
SAVED BY THE BELL

FAMOUS FOR **RAPID AND SUDDEN WEIGHT LOSS**
AFTER A FEW YEARS IN THE JOB

On the face of it, Screech, the mascot of the Washington Nationals MLB team, is a perfectly standard mascot. He's an animal with curiously human features, such as arms, legs on which he can stand upright and, by the looks of things, opposable thumbs too. He's fuzzy and furry, and wears the uniform of the team he represents, cap and all.

But the difference with Screech is the mouth. And the eyes. Both are always open. Both are always wide. Both are fixed, dead, not to be altered or closed. Both could convey any number of emotions, from 'YES! I AM EXCITED! SPORTS! SPORTS! SPORTS!' to 'I have seen things you wouldn't believe . . . awful things . . . life-changing things . . .'

The other notable thing about Screech is that, when he 'hatched' on the field in 2005, he was quite a tubby little bird, with at least one spare tyre around that waist in the traditional manner of the cuddly mascot. But in 2009 he was reimagined, reappearing as the svelte figure we see today, possibly after a winter in the gym, possibly after hitting the Atkins diet, possibly after some sort of awful wasting disease. We're all for encouraging the kids to be healthy, but the idea that a team has fat-shamed their mascot does seem a step too far.

NAME **PHANG**

TEAM **PHILADELPHIA UNION**

SPORT **FOOTBALL**

YEARS ACTIVE **2018–PRESENT**

STYLE **PHUN, PHUNKY AND SIMPLY REFUSES TO USE THE LETTER 'F'**

FAMOUS FOR **BEING A SNAKE WHO GREW ARMS AND LEGS THANKS TO LIGHTNING**

The Philadelphia Union MLS team have been around since 2010 but spent the first eight years of their existence without a mascot. In the city of the Phillie Phanatic, Gritty and Franklin the Dog, they looked a little behind the times. So in 2018, enter . . . Phang.

Naturally, questions arose as to how a snake, creatures who famously do not have arms or legs, had arms and legs. But do not worry, they had an answer for that: born a 'normal' snake, apparently Phang wanted more than the usual snake life of eating mice whole, slithering around and so forth, and so desperate was he to play soccer that he took a ball and a pair of boots out onto the Union pitch, tied them together, gripped the middle of the string and 'waited for lightning to strike'. When it did, it fused his snakiness with some human DNA on the boots, and by happy coincidence it was the 'arms and legs' bits of human DNA rather than, say, 'the appendix' or 'bits of hair inside your ear that you can't get out with even the most delicate tweezers'.

In fairness to them, the Union have at least tried to offer a little history and education in the story of Phang. Apparently his great, great, great, great, great-grandfather was the snake upon which Benjamin Franklin based his famous 1754 *Join, or Die* cartoon, in which Phang Snr Snr Snr Snr Snr Snr Snr was sliced into eight pieces to represent the disunited union in America at the time. This story also tests the theory that kids will believe absolutely anything you tell them if you use a human–animal hybrid.

SILENCES

And finally – mascots observing moments of silence

Fred the Red, Manchester United's mascot, who in his spare time helps kids learn their times tables via the medium of a techno-backed dance video for the BBC.

Bolton's Lofty the Lion, who in 2003 released an 80s hair metal-style single called 'Let's Rock This Town'. It did not trouble the charts.

Kingsley Royal, who was once sent off during a Premier League game for 'confusing the officials', and Queensley Royal, who appeared in 2012 as Kingsley Royal's love interest, celebrated their romance in the most natural way possible: by having a lawnmower race down the side of the pitch.

Billy Bantam of Bradford, who is one of a number of mascots to star on the Nickelodeon show Nick Kicks, in which contestants have to negotiate a ball pool then score as many penalties as possible.

Lobby, the mascot of Japanese football team Cerezo Osaka, who has to cope with the indignity of his mother – Madame Lobina – following him around at games.

Jaxson de Ville of the Jaxonville Jaguars, who got in trouble with the authorities so many times that he spent one game in 2007 in a cage by the side of the field.

PICTURE ACKNOWLEDGEMENTS

p6 Stuart MacFarlane/Arsenal FC via Getty Images; **p10** Adam Glanzman/Getty Images; **p15** Len Redkoles/NHLI via Getty Images; **p17** Clive Mason/Getty Images; **p18** Larry French/Getty Images; **p21** Daniel Hambury/EMPICS Sport/PA Images; **p23** John Angelillo/UPI/PA Images; **p24** Steve Drew/EMPICS Sport/PA Images; **p26** Joe Robbins/Getty Images; **p29** Pete Norton/Getty Images; **p31** Sean Gardner/ Getty Images; **p32** Dan Mullan/Getty Images; **p34** Giulio Napolitano/AFP/Getty Images; **p37** © 2017 NBAE Photo by Brock Williams-Smith/Getty Images; **p39** Matthew Ashton/EMPICS Sport/PA Images; **p40** Focus on Sport/ Getty Images; **p45** Chris Graythen/Getty Images; **p47** Pete Norton/Getty Images; **p48** © 2007 NBAE Photo by David Dow/Getty Images; **p50** Etsuo Hara/Getty Images; **p53** Hwang Kwang-Mo/AFP/ Getty Images; **p54** Allsport AUS /Allsport/Getty Images; **p57** Brad Mangin/Sports Illustrated/Getty Images; **p59** Rolf Vennenbernd/DPA/PA Images; **p60** Kendall Shaw/ CSM/Alamy Live News; **p63** Gabriel Piko/PikoPress/PA Images; **p64** Stephen McCarthy/ Sportsfile via Getty Images; **p67** © 2017 NBAE Photo by Fernando Medina/NBAE via Getty Images; **p68** Steve Mitchell/EMPICS Sport/PA Images; **p73** Etsuo Hara/Getty Images; **p74** David Woodley/Action Plus via Getty Images; **p77** Thomas Starke/ Bongarts/Getty Images; **p79** Ethan Miller/Getty Images; **p80** The Asahi Shimbun via Getty Images; **p83** David E Klutho/Sports Illustrated/Getty Images; **p84** Matthew Lewis/Getty Images; **p87** Doug Murray/Zuma Press/PA Images; **p89** USA TODAY Sports/SIPA USA/PA Images; **p90** PA/PA Archive/PA Images; **p92** Kevin Abele/Icon Sportswire via Getty Images; **p95** Seth Sanchez/Icon Sportswire/Corbis via Getty Images; **p96** PRiME Media Images/Alamy Live News; **p100** Richard Heathcote/Getty Images; **p102** John Walton/EMPICS Sport/PA Images; **p104** Randy Belice/NBAE via Getty Images; **p107** Joe Robbins/Getty Images; **p109** Jeff Holmes/Press Association Images; **p110** © 2006 NBAE Photo by Jeff Reinking/NBAE via Getty Images; **p113** Stephen Pond/EMPICS Sport/PA Images; **p114** Brian Blanco/Getty Images; **p116** Brian Bahr /Allsport/ Getty Images; **p118** Michael Wade/Icon Sportswire via Getty Images; **p121** Chuck Myers/ABACA USA/PA Images; **p123** Ricky Fitchett/Zuma Press/PA Images; **p124** Shaun Botterill/Getty Images; **p125** (top) Paul Ellis/AFP/Getty Images; **p125** (bottom) Nigel Keene/ProSports/Shutterstock; **p126** (top) John Walton/ EMPICS Sport/PA Images; **p126** (bottom) Etsuo Hara/Getty Images; **p127** Jamie McDonald/Getty Images.